"Massimo Faggioli's superb new biography is the best short introduction to John XXIII around. Concise, well-researched and beautifully written, it is the perfect invitation to come to know the remarkable saint who invited some fresh air into the Catholic church."

—James Martin, SJ
  Author of *My Life with the Saints*

"*John XXIII: The Medicine of Mercy* is healing balm for the soul. This fine book sets forth the surprising twists and turns of a son of an Italian farmer whose 'north star' always was responding with compassion and obedience to the real needs of people. Even his 20 years in 'exile' in diplomatic posts in Bulgaria and Turkey became nourishment for his spiritual life. Pope John's story can lead us into our own deep listening to the Spirit among us."

—Simone Campbell, SSS
  Executive Director NETWORK, Washington, DC

"Professor Faggioli's readable account of the humble journey of Pope St. John XXIII shows what a gift to the church Roncalli was: A man of simple devotion to the liturgy and to Scripture, a man who heard and saw the signs of the times, a man whose style and substance paved the way for Pope Francis. Roncalli's motto was 'obedience and peace.' Faggioli shows how the saint's unwavering obedience brought him peace in very difficult circumstances and taught him that peace on earth is possible in obedient devotion to the reign of God."

—Terrence W. Tilley
  Avery Cardinal Dulles, S.J., Chair in Catholic Theology,
    Fordham University

"Faggioli has produced the first biography in English based largely on the recently completed edition of Roncalli's extensive diaries. He is able therefore to trace the external events in Roncalli's life in a newly reliable way but, more important, also to reveal the pope's internal journey from a naive peasant boy into one of the world's most respected and beloved leaders."

—John O'Malley, SJ
  Georgetown University

People of God

Remarkable Lives, Heroes of Faith

People of God is a series of inspiring biographies for the general reader. Each volume offers a compelling and honest narrative of the life of an important twentieth- or twenty-first-century Catholic. Some living and some now deceased, each of these women and men has known challenges and weaknesses familiar to most of us but responded to them in ways that call us to our own forms of heroism. Each offers a credible and concrete witness of faith, hope, and love to people of our own day.

John XXIII	Massimo Faggioli
Oscar Romero	Kevin Clarke
Thomas Merton	Michael W. Higgins
Megan Rice	Dennis Coday
Francis	Michael Collins
Flannery O'Connor	Angela O'Donnell
Martin Sheen	Rose Pacatte
Jean Vanier	Michael W. Higgins
Dorothy Day	Patrick Jordan
Luis Antonio Tagle	Cindy Wooden

More titles to follow

John XXIII

The Medicine of Mercy

Massimo Faggioli

LITURGICAL PRESS

Collegeville, Minnesota

www.litpress.org

Library of Congress Control Number: 2014930906

ISBN 978-0-8146-4951-0

Contents

Abbreviations   vii

Acknowledgments   xi

Introduction   1

Chapter One
The Young Angelo Giuseppe (1881–1904)   11

Chapter Two
Dangerous Times: Antimodernism, World War, and
Curia Politics (1905–1924)   29

Chapter Three
Learning from the East: Papal Diplomat in Bulgaria
and Turkey (1925–1944)   51

Chapter Four
Between the "Exile" and the Final Ascent: France
and Venice (1945–1958)   79

Chapter Five
A Pope of Temporary Transition with a Robust Program:
Rome (1958–1963)   105

Conclusion
John XXIII: Medicine of Mercy and Signs of
the Times   133

Selected Bibliography   141

Index   147

Abbreviations

ASV   Archivio Segreto Vaticano, Città del Vaticano: *Archivio della Delegazione Apostolica in Bulgaria* (32 folders), and *Affari Ecclesiastici Straordinari* (AES), Bulgaria, Indice IV (periodo), 2 (23 folders).

Il Giornale dell'Anima   *Edizione nazionale dei diari di Angelo Giuseppe Roncalli–Giovanni XXIII. Vol. 1: Il Giornale dell'Anima: Soliloqui, note e diari spirituali.* By Angelo Giuseppe Roncalli/Pope John XXIII. Edited by Alberto Melloni. (Bologna: Istituto per le scienze religiose, Fondazione per le scienze religiose Giovanni XXIII, 2003.

Diaries 1905–1925   *Edizione nazionale dei diari di Angelo Giuseppe Roncalli–Giovanni XXIII. Vol. 2: Nelle mani di Dio a servizio dell'uomo: I diari di don Roncalli, 1905–1925.* By Angelo Giuseppe Roncalli/Pope John XXIII. Edited by Lucia Butturini. (Bologna: Istituto per le scienze religiose, Fondazione per le scienze religiose Giovanni XXIII, 2008.)

Diaries Bulgaria *Edizione nazionale dei diari di Angelo*
1925–1934   *Giuseppe Roncalli–Giovanni XXIII.*
                  Vol. 3: Tener da conto: Agendine di
                  Bulgaria, 1925–1934. By Angelo
                  Giuseppe Roncalli/Pope John XXIII.
                  Edited by Massimo Faggioli. (Bologna:
                  Istituto per le scienze religiose, Fonda-
                  zione per le scienze religiose Giovanni
                  XXIII, 2008.)

Diaries Turkey–Greece *Edizione nazionale dei diari di Angelo*
1935–1939   *Giuseppe Roncalli–Giovanni XXIII.*
                        Vol. 4.1: La mia vita in Oriente:
                        Agende del delegato apostolico, 1935–
                        1939. Edited by Valeria Martano. (Bo-
                        logna: Istituto per le scienze religiose,
                        Fondazione per le scienze religiose
                        Giovanni XXIII, 2006.)

Diaries Turkey–Greece *Edizione nazionale dei diari di Angelo*
1940–1944   *Giuseppe Roncalli–Giovanni XXIII.*
                        Vol. 4.2: La mia vita in Oriente:
                        Agende del delegato apostolico, 1940–
                        1944. Edited by Valeria Martano. (Bo-
                        logna: Istituto per le scienze religiose,
                        Fondazione per le scienze religiose
                        Giovanni XXIII, 2008.)

Diaries France *Edizione nazionale dei diari di Angelo*
1945–1948   *Giuseppe Roncalli–Giovanni XXIII.*
                  Vol. 5.1: Anni di Francia: Agende del
                  nunzio, 1945–1948. Edited by Étienne
                  Fouilloux. (Bologna: Istituto per le
                  scienze religiose, Fondazione per le

scienze religiose Giovanni XXIII,
2004.)

Diaries France *1949–1953*	*Edizione nazionale dei diari di Angelo* *Giuseppe Roncalli–Giovanni XXIII.* *Vol. 5.2: Anni di Francia: Agende del* *nunzio, 1949–1953.* Edited by Étienne Fouilloux. (Bologna: Istituto per le scienze religiose, Fondazione per le scienze religiose Giovanni XXIII, 2006.)
Diaries Venice *1953–1955*	*Edizione nazionale dei diari di Angelo* *Giuseppe Roncalli–Giovanni XXIII.* *Vol. 6.1: Pace e Vangelo: Agende del* *patriarca, 1953–1955.* Edited by Enrico Galavotti. (Bologna: Istituto per le scienze religiose, Fondazione per le scienze religiose Giovanni XXIII, 2008.)
Diaries Venice *1956–1958*	*Edizione nazionale dei diari di Angelo* *Giuseppe Roncalli–Giovanni XXIII.* *Vol. 6.2: Pace e Vangelo: Agende del* *patriarca, 1956–1958.* Edited by Enrico Galavotti. (Bologna: Istituto per le scienze religiose, Fondazione per le scienze religiose Giovanni XXIII, 2008.)
Diaries Pontificate *1958–1963*	*Edizione nazionale dei diari di Angelo* *Giuseppe Roncalli–Giovanni XXIII.* *Vol. 7: Pater amabilis: Agende del* *pontefice, 1958–1963.* Edited by Mauro Velati. (Bologna: Istituto per le scienze religiose, Fondazione per le

scienze religiose Giovanni XXIII,
2007. Pp. xxxvii, 569.)

History of Vatican II   *History of Vatican II*, vols. 1–5, ed.
Giuseppe Alberigo, English version ed.
Joseph A. Komonchak (Maryknoll,
NY: Orbis, 1995–2006).

Predicazione a Istanbul   Angelo G. Roncalli (Giovanni XXIII),
*La predicazione a Istanbul. Omelie,
discorsi e note pastorali (1935–1944)*,
ed. Alberto Melloni (Firenze: Olschki,
1993).

All the translations are the author's except where otherwise
indicated.

Acknowledgments

This book is the result of my long-lasting interest in John XXIII that took concrete shape in the year 2007–2008 for the edition of the "little notes" of Angelo Giuseppe Roncalli in Bulgaria (1925–1934). The research was made possible by the release in September 2006 of documents of the Apostolic Delegation in Bulgaria in the Vatican Secret Archives.[1] The book was conceived during the fiftieth anniversary of Vatican II and written in 2013, a year of particular importance for the Catholic Church. It completes and complements my research on the history and theology Vatican II as the key to understand the church of today.

This short biography of Angelo Giuseppe Roncalli/John XXIII owes much to the seminal work done by my mentors and colleagues at the Fondazione per le scienze religiose Giovanni XXIII in Bologna, where I did research between 1996 and 2008. First of all, I want to recognize Giuseppe Alberigo (1926–2007) who introduced me to this field of

---

1. Angelo Giuseppe Roncalli/Pope John XXIII, *Edizione nazionale dei diari di Angelo Giuseppe Roncalli–Giovanni XXIII. Vol. 3: Tener da conto: Agendine di Bulgaria, 1925–1934.* Ed. Massimo Faggioli (Bologna: Istituto per le scienze religiose, Fondazione per le scienze religiose Giovanni XXIII, 2008).

study in his church history course at the University of Bologna in the academic year 1991–1992 and after that involved me with the team doing research for the five-volume *History of Vatican II* between 1995 and 2001. Others deserving recognition include Alberto Melloni, who has done seminal work on the papers of Angelo Giuseppe Roncalli, beginning in the 1980s with the first scholarly edition of the *Giornale dell'Anima*; Giuseppe Ruggieri for his groundbreaking reflections on the theology of Roncalli; Federico Ruozzi for the pioneering work of the video historical sources for the history of John XXIII and Vatican II; and Enrico Galavotti for his labor for the complete edition of the private diaries of Angelo Giuseppe Roncalli/John XXIII, accomplished in ten volumes between 2003 and 2008 thanks to the acriby of the editors of the other volumes, Lucia Butturini, Étienne Fouilloux, Mauro Velati, and to the editorial expertise of Gianstefano Riva and Paolo Albertazzi. This treasure of personal notes of the future pope of Vatican II (published in Italian and not translated into English, except for a previous edition of *Journal of a Soul*) are key to this book in the attempt to gather and translate the best of the scholarly works on Roncalli from the last three decades and to reinterpret John XXIII in the context of the Catholic Church fifty years after Vatican II.

The historical studies of these last three decades are crucial for understanding not just the life of Angelo Giuseppe Roncalli, but modern Catholicism in general, and especially the particular role of the papacy in the global church and in a global world. This scholarly research has resonated in a particular way in these last few months with the election of Pope Francis on March 13, 2013. For this reason this book is the fruit of personal encounters during this last unforgettable year, when I had several occasions to speak about

Vatican II and Pope John XXIII, in particular in a series of most enjoyable public events at various venues in New York City. Here I want to thank the friends and colleagues that made those events possible: Chris Bellitto, James McCartin, Sr. Simone Campbell, Drew Christiansen, SJ, David Gibson, Natalia Imperatori-Lee, and Terrence Tilley.

My "Jesuit connections" in America have been a large part of the work I managed to accomplish during my first six years in the United States. Thanks to John Baldovin, SJ, Daniel Madigan, SJ, James Martin, SJ, and David Schultenover, SJ, and especially to John O'Malley, SJ, and Mark Massa, SJ. Other colleagues are an essential part of this new conversation of which I have been a part since the summer of 2008, when I moved to America: Kevin Ahern, John Borelli, Thomas Cattoi, Kathleen Cummings, Robin Darling Young, E. J. Dionne Jr., Richard Gaillardetz, Patrick Hayes, Tom Heneghan, Cathleen Kaveny, Gerard Mannion, Tim Matovina, John McGreevy, Robert Orsi, Anthony Ruff, OSB, Maureen Sullivan, OP, and Terry Tilley.

Liturgical Press encouraged me to "seize the moment" in the spring of 2013; I thank Hans Christoffersen and Barry Hudock for their initiative and encouragement. I thank also the many good colleagues at the University of St. Thomas (St. Paul, MN) in the theology department and my students who continue to be fundamental for my rediscovery of the relevance of key themes and figures in church history and in the history of theology.

This short biography is an opportunity, in light of the signs of our times, to better understand Roncalli's life: missions, travels, contacts, spiritual life—which contributed to a turning point in the history of modern Catholicism. Much of that has to do with the fact that Angelo Giuseppe Roncalli/ John XXIII expanded the horizons of his worldview by living almost thirty years outside of Italy in Bulgaria, Turkey, and France. Every biographical work is to some extent, consciously or unconsciously, also autobiographical. For this reason, this book is dedicated to my teachers and mentors in Ferrara, Bologna, at the Monastic Community of Bose, in Tübingen, Boston, and Washington, DC.

Minneapolis, January 25, 2014
Fifty-fifth Anniversary of the Calling of the
Second Vatican Council

Introduction

Making Popes Saints

The year 2014 marks an important date in the history of the Catholic Church and of the papacy with the canonization by Pope Francis of two of his closest predecessors on the chair of Peter: John XXIII (1958–1963) and John Paul II (1978–2005). John XXIII, the pope who called Vatican II in 1959, and John Paul II, who was a bishop at Vatican II, are proclaimed *saints* of the Catholic Church on the same day and during the fiftieth anniversary celebration of Vatican II (2012–2015). For both popes, the final decision regarding their canonization follows what church historian Enrico Galavotti, in his masterful book on the Roncalli trial, called the "shadow canonization" effect[1]—a canonization already sanctioned by the people, waiting for the decision of the Vatican "saint factory" in the Roman Curia.[2]

---

1. Enrico Galavotti, *Processo a papa Giovanni. La causa di canonizzazione di A.G. Roncalli (1965–2000)* (Bologna, Italy: il Mulino, 2005), 439.

2. See Kenneth L. Woodward, *Making Saints: How the Catholic Church Determines Who Becomes a Saint, Who Doesn't, and Why* (New York: Simon & Schuster, 1990).

As a Catholic and a historian, Angelo Giuseppe Roncalli took seriously the role of the saints and popes, particularly the popes of modern church history who had been proclaimed saints, such as Pius X (canonized by Pius XII in 1954). Both Pius X and John XXIII belong to a sense of Catholicism that accepts the idea of a pope being proclaimed a saint, which has not always been typical of the Catholic Church. Paradoxically, it was only after the pontificate of Pius X, the pope who in 1907 launched the purge against theological "modernism," that this modern phenomenon has become part of the theological and public understanding of the papacy.

At the end of 2013, 81 of the 263 predecessors of Pope Benedict XVI were regarded by the church as saints. Of these 81 popes, 47 of them were among the first 48 successors of Peter; half of these 47 "popes/saints" were martyrs and died before the year 500.[3] The most recent popes to be canonized in the modern era before Pius X in 1954 were Pius V in 1712 and Gregory VII in 1726. After Gregory VII (1073–1085) and until the year 2000, only three popes were canonized (Celestin V, Pius V, and Pius X), and only eight have been beatified.[4]

The change in practice for canonization and beatification relates to the theological and cultural changes involving the Roman papacy—the "mystique of the papacy."[5] For almost

---

3. Ibid., 281. Of the thirty-three popes after Peter considered "martyrs," we now know most of them died natural deaths. See John O'Malley, *A History of the Popes: From Peter to the Present* (Lanham MD: Sheed and Ward, 2009) and Eamon Duffy, *Saints & Sinners. A History of the Popes* (New Haven, CT: Yale University Press, 1997).

4. For the process for Celestine V and Pius V, see Galavotti, *Processo a papa Giovanni*, 31.

5. Massimo Faggioli, "Something Lost . . . and Gained. The Mystique of the Papacy after Benedict's Departure," *The Tablet*, 2 (March 2013): 10–11.

every pope of the nineteenth and twentieth centuries, starting with Pius IX, the process for beatification has been opened. The results have been diverse: Pius X was canonized in 1954 and Innocent XI (1676–1689) in 1956.[6] During the last fourteen years alone three popes—Pius IX, John XXIII, and John Paul II—have been beatified (the first two in 2000, the third in 2011), and John XXIII and John Paul II were canonized by Pope Francis in 2014. For more than two centuries no pope was canonized; during the last fourteen years (2000–2014) there have been three beatifications of recent popes and two canonizations in 2014.[7] The process of beatification has been opened for Pius XII, Paul VI, and John Paul I.[8] For the first time in history, there was the beatification of a pope, John Paul II, by Joseph Ratzinger/Benedict XVI, his immediate successor (and his theologian-in-chief in the Roman Curia for twenty-five years).

Almost twenty-five years ago in his description of the "saints-making machine," Kenneth Woodward argued that papal causes present special problems. First, papal causes are only introduced by another pope. Second, the published

---

6. The process of beatification for Innocent was introduced in 1741 by Benedict XIV. The canonization of Innocent XI "savior of Christendom" by Pius XII in 1956 played a role in the Cold War era confrontation with Communism portrayed as the "new Islam." See *Diaries Venice 1956–1958* (October 7, 1956), 224.

7. Beatification was once called "semicanonizatio," the authorization of a cult at the local level, even if the distinction was clear already in the Middle Ages.

8. Pius XII's cause of canonization was opened on November 18, 1965, by Paul VI. John Paul II opened the process for Paul VI in 1993 and for John Paul I in 2003. In the recent history of the papacy after Vatican I, among the last ten popes, only Leo XIII, Benedict XV, and Pius XI have so far been excluded from this process.

writings of a pope are not subject to the usual preliminary
scrutiny by theological censors. Third, popes generate much
more written material that postulators are expected to examine, but which they examine only in part—even in complicated cases like Pius XII's. Fourth, "unlike most saints,
popes tend to make many enemies. . . . Thus no papal
cause, especially that of a controversial figure like John or
Pius, is apt to move quickly as long as any of his opponents
remain alive and influential in the church." Fifth, "a pope
must be judged not only on his personal holiness but also
on his stewardship as supreme teacher and head of the
church," as the manual published by Benedict XIV (1740–
1758), *De canonizatione sanctorum*, explained clearly.[9]

Woodward's description of possible problems says much
about Saint John XXIII. On October 28, 1963, at the Second
Vatican Council, prominent cardinals such as Giacomo
Lercaro, cardinal of Bologna, and Leo Jozef Suenens, cardinal of Mechelen-Bruxelles, famously proposed John XXIII,
the pope who called Vatican II and who died during the first
intersession of the council in June 1963, for an ancient "conciliar canonization."[10] But Paul VI waited two years, until
November 18, 1965, before making public his decision to
open a "normal" process of beatification for John XXIII
together with the process for Pius XII. This decision tied

9. Woodward, *Making Saints*, 288. See also Miguel Gotor, *I beati
del papa. Santità, Inquisizione e obbedienza in età moderna* (Florence,
Italy: Olschki, 2002).

10. It is worth remembering that the speech of cardinal Leo Jozef
Suenens was never included in the multivolume "corpus" of the official documents (*Acta Synodalia*) of Vatican II edited by Roman
Curia officials. See Alberto Melloni, "La causa Roncalli: origini di un
processo canonico," *Cristianesimo nella Storia*, XVIII/3 (1997): 607–
36; Galavotti, *Processo a papa Giovanni*, 58–77.

together at least three purposes: "a beatification by acclamation was avoided . . . John XXIII and Pius XII were associated as links in the Roman continuity . . . [and] the two popes were placed in the service of the post-conciliar period and of the aggiornamento as revised by Paul VI."[11] Paul VI's move "put a definitive end to the movement that took off right after John's death for the council to canonize him by acclamation."[12]

"They were using John [XXIII] to get at Pius [XII]," as Fr. Paolo Molinari, postulator to the cause of Pius XII, put it.[13] But many believed that in the pairing of Pius XII and John XXIII, one would make impossible the canonization of the other. The paths of these two causes took different directions, despite the intention of Paul VI to tie them together, mostly due to the impact of the debate on the pontificate of Pius XII during World War II and his decision (made consciously) not to publicly denounce the Holocaust of the Jews carried out by the Nazis, with whom he had signed a concordat in Germany in 1933 as a papal nuncio.[14] While the process for Pius XII stalled until very recently,[15] the process for John XXIII advanced for many reasons. The collapse of Soviet communism in 1989–1991 put an end to

11. Christoph Theobald, "The Church under the Word of God," *History of Vatican II*, vol. V: 362.

12. John W. O'Malley, *What Happened at Vatican II* (Cambridge, MA: Belknap Press of Harvard University Press, 2008), 283.

13. Woodward, *Making Saints*, 285.

14. Roberto Rusconi, *Santo Padre. La santità del papa da San Pietro a Giovanni Paolo II* (Rome: Viella, 2010), 496–530.

15. On December 19, 2009, Benedict XVI acknowledged the "heroic virtues" of Pius XII and declared him "venerable," based on the recommendation of the committee. John Paul II was declared "venerable" on the same day.

the conspiracy-minded speculations about the communist sympathies of John XXIII for the Soviet Union. A second element was the impatience of John Paul II with the canonical procedures in general; a third element, especially important, was the development of the reception of Vatican II. During the pontificate of John Paul II, Vatican II rose to the status of a "providential event." John Paul II, the last pope who had been a council father, defined Vatican II as a "compass" for the Catholic Church.

Making John XXIII a Saint

It is important to examine the canonization of John XXIII, the pope who convened Vatican II, in the context of the church at the beginning of the twenty-first century. On the one hand, the canonization became part of the debate on Vatican II, and it survived the attempt of some in the church to minimize Vatican II and to indict the pope who called it.[16] On the other hand, the canonization of the pope of *aggiornamento* could not count on a powerful religious order (such as Opus Dei for Escrivà de Balaguer, who was beatified in 1992 and proclaimed saint in 2002), nor on a new Catholic movement for the beginning of the process (such as the Focolare Movement for John Paul II), nor on a coherent Curia group of insiders (such as the archconservative milieu around Msgr. Piolanti and the Pontifical Lateran University for Pius IX).[17] After the worldwide broadcasted stunt of the *Santo subito!* banner in

16. Massimo Faggioli, *Vatican II: The Battle for Meaning* (New York: Paulist Press, 2012).

17. See Galavotti, *Processo a papa Giovanni*, 425–29. The process for Pius IX's beatification was begun on February 11, 1907, and re-commenced three times.

St. Peter's Square immediately after John Paul II's death, the process for him followed a normal path but with an accelerated pace;[18] nevertheless, Benedict XVI did not choose to promote the canonization of his predecessor *ex certa scientia*, which is exactly what Pope Francis decided to do for John XXIII with his decision announced on July 5, 2013.

Within the context of these new trends, the canonization of a pope is an eminent act of church politics (and not only for the Catholic Church if we think about the canonization in the year 2000 by the Orthodox Church of the Romanov family, killed by the Bolsheviks in 1918), more than the beatification or canonization of "normal" saints.[19] The double beatification of Pius IX and John XXIII in 2000 was undoubtedly aimed at balancing different interpretations of the relationship between Vatican II and the change in the church during the twentieth century. It took ninety-three years to beatify Pius IX, thirty-five for John XXIII, and only six for John Paul II. It took longer for John XXIII, despite the fact that many council fathers wanted to canonize him at Vatican II following an ancient procedure.

The beatification and canonization of a pope by another pope is the ultimate phase in a long history of the centralization of the politics of sainthood in Rome. It is the final moment of a history that began in the eleventh century from a situation in which the consensus of locally elected bishops was necessary for establishing the sainthood of a pope, to the situation of today where the consensus of the pope is the only necessary element for making both bishops and

---

18. But not as fast as other processes, like St. Anthony of Padua (canonized in 1232 less than a year after his death) and St. Francis of Assisi (canonized 18 months after his death).

19. See Woodward, *Making Saints*, 280.

saints.[20] With the joint canonization of John XXIII and John Paul II in 2014, Pope Francis elevated two of his close predecessors. One of the challenges for Catholicism is to reconcile this tendency of proclaiming popes saints with Pope Francis's clear view of the papacy as a humble ministry serving the church. But it is also clear that the pair of John XXIII and John Paul II canonized by Pope Francis is significantly different from the pair of John XXIII and Pius IX beatified in 2000 by John Paul II—and much different from the other pair in the pipeline of the "saint factory" in the early 2000s, John XXIII and Pius XII.

In the spring of 2011, when Benedict XVI announced the beatification of John Paul II, the journal *Foreign Policy* published an article on the miracle required for a beatification, with the subtitle "Some Theology, a Little Science, and a Whole Lot of Politics."[21] This is true for many popes who were proclaimed saints. Since early church history, the sainthood of the pope became a necessary requisite for the new "legal" understanding of the see of Rome in light of the principle *prima sedes a nemine iudicatur* (nobody can judge the see of Rome): "If the bishop of Rome was exempted from every kind of ecclesiastical judgment it was at least possible to conclude that he could not sin, or at least not seriously, and that he had received, along with his office, the promise that he would remain holy."[22]

20. See Rusconi, *Santo Padre*, 40.

21. Joshua E. Keating, "How Does the Vatican Decide What's a Miracle?" *Foreign Policy* (January 14, 2011), http://www.foreignpolicy.com/articles/2011/01/14/how_does_the_vatican_decide_what_s_a_miracle.

22. Klaus Schatz, *Papal Primacy. From Its Origins to the Present* (Collegeville, MN: Liturgical Press, 1996), 88.

The situation of John XXIII is different from any other pope beatified and canonized: "The fame of sanctity of Roncalli resembles that of Wojtyla for its timeliness, but not for its content."[23] The fame of sainthood of John XXIII has always been universal and global, in the Catholic Church as well as in cultural and spiritual milieus very distant from the official Catholic one. This is not because John XXIII was the first pope of television. German-American and Jewish political thinker Hannah Arendt saw in John XXIII the realization of the possibility of "a Christian pope"—a pope whose faith witness was more important than the monarchical-imperial elements of the papal *aura*.[24] The Italian writer, filmmaker, and public intellectual Pier Paolo Pasolini (arguably

23. Alberto Melloni, *Papa Giovanni. Un cristiano e il suo concilio* (Turin, Italy: Einaudi, 2009), 8.

24. Hannah Arendt, "The Christian Pope," *New York Review of Books* (June 17, 1965), a review article of *The Journal of a Soul* (translated by Dorothy White and published in English by McGraw-Hill, 1965): "For pages and pages it [*The Journal of a Soul*] reads like an elementary textbook on how to be good and to avoid evil. And yet in its own strange and unfamiliar way, it succeeds in giving a clear answer to two questions [that] were in the minds of many people when, two years ago, 'Angelo Giuseppe Roncalli who took the name of John XXIII' lay dying. They were very simply and unequivocally brought to my own attention by a Roman chambermaid: 'Madam,' she said, 'this Pope was a real Christian. How could that be? And how could it happen that a true Christian would sit on St. Peter's chair? Didn't he first have to be appointed Bishop, and Archbishop, and Cardinal, until he finally was elected to be Pope? Had nobody been aware of who he was?' Well, the answer to the last of her three questions seems to be 'No.'" Arendt's essay was republished in Arendt, *Men in Dark Times* (New York: Harcourt, 1968, 57–69) and recently as a book in Italian with the title *Il papa cristiano. Umanità e fede in Giovanni XXIII* (Bologna, Italy: EDB, 2013).

the last non-Catholic prophetic voice in contemporary Italy) dedicated his movie *The Gospel According to St. Matthew* (1964) "to the dear, joyous, familiar memory of Pope John XXIII" who had died a few months before.[25]

The fame of sainthood for John XXIII has not been damaged these last fifty years because more is known about him than any other pope in church history. Through his private journal, which has been used for this biographical study, the daily life path of Angelo Giuseppe Roncalli/John XXIII has been rebuilt with a degree of accuracy and depth that is not available for any other pope.[26]

25. About Pasolini and John XXIII, see "Marxismo e Cristian-esimo," lecture given by Pasolini in Brescia on December 13, 1964, published in *L'Eco di Brescia*, December 18, 1964, and recently in Pier Paolo Pasolini, *Saggi sulla politica e la società*, Walter Siti and Silvia De Laude, eds. (Milan, Italy: Mondadori, 1999), 787–824: "John XXIII performed the highly democratic act chuckling at the thought of himself in authority. . . . John XXIII accomplished, in his short pontificate, a profound revolution in the Church" (795).

26. Giuseppe Alberigo, "Roncalli 'privato'?" *Revisitare Giovanni XXIII*, Enrico Galavotti, ed., Cristianesimo nella Storia, XXV/2 (2004): 457–79.

CHAPTER ONE

The Young Angelo Giuseppe

(1881–1904)

Young Catholic in a Young Italy

Angelo Giuseppe Roncalli was born on November 25, 1881, in the village of Sotto il Monte (literally "under the mountain"), which is ten miles from Bergamo and thirty-five miles northeast of Milan, in Northern Italy. He was the fourth of thirteen children with an extended family of more than thirty members. He was baptized the day of his birth by the village pastor, Don Francesco Rebuzzini, whose sudden death Angelo Giuseppe would witness in 1898, when he was a seventeen-year-old seminarian.

Angelo Giuseppe's family shaped his spiritual habits, and he stayed in close touch with them his whole life. His parents, Giovanni Battista and Marianna Mazzola, were married in 1877. They lived a very frugal life, sometimes close to poverty, as was typical of peasants working the land owned by somebody else—in their case the rich Morlani family from Bergamo. Angelo's father was a *mezzadro*, a sharecropper, and the land worked by the Roncalli family was not very productive: polenta and soup were on the family's table more often than bread, bread being the food for more affluent people in Italy at that time.

Angelo Giuseppe Roncalli belonged to the first generation of Italians born in the new Kingdom of Italy, which was unified by the dynasty of Savoy (formerly ruling from Turin over the kingdom of Piedmont and Sardinia) during a five-decades-long series of wars of independence called the "Risorgimento"—the resurgence of the Italian nation after centuries of domination by other European powers and the papacy. The new Kingdom of Italy, proclaimed in 1861, conquered its new capital, Rome, in 1870 during the celebration of the (first) Vatican Council under Pius IX. This new Italy was being built at the expense of the Papal States of the last "Pope King" Pius IX and at the expense (financially, politically, and culturally) of the Catholic Church. From 1870 until 1929, all the popes saw themselves as "prisoners in the Vatican"—deprived of their sovereignty as a political entity. The new Regno d'Italia "secularized," that is, incorporated, many properties of the church and banned the teaching of theology from state universities (the only ones existing on Italian soil). Until the beginning of the twentieth century, popes and bishops did not acknowledge the moral and legal legitimacy of the new state.[1]

Bergamo was in the region of Lombardia, one of the so-called "white regions" of Italy, where Catholicism had been particularly shaped by the Council of Trent since the time of Saint Charles Borromeo (1538–1584, archbishop of Milan 1560–1584). Catholicism in Bergamo also was

---

1. Giovanni Miccoli, *Tra mito della cristianità e secolarizzazione* (Casale Monferrato, Italy: Marietti, 1985).

shaped by a committed "social Catholicism" made of workers unions, Catholic credit banks, and the first Catholic-democratic politicians in an Italy run by secularist and anticlerical politicians. Milan was considered the "second Catholic capital" of Italy and was a proud example of an intellectual approach to religion and the church—certainly not less intellectual than the Rome of the popes. It was the center of the beginning of a new Italy and also for the relationship between the central Catholic Church in Rome and the rest of Italy. Catholicism was still pondering the effects of the Vatican Council (1869–1870), but Catholics in Italy were not the reactionaries and "ultramontanists" the Vatican wanted them to be; they were cautiously opening up to modern times and its challenges. It was during this time when many Italians (196,000 in the year 1888 alone) migrated abroad (many to the United States) looking for work.

"I Am Far from Being an Angel"

Roncalli was in touch with this devout and traditional practice of Catholicism. At the same time, he was well-read and influenced by his great-uncle Zaverio Roncalli (brother of his grandfather), from whom he received the first elements of a traditional Christian education. Catholicism in the Roncalli family was solid and conventional, in a country and region where everybody was a "cradle Catholic" and religious diversity was not part of the landscape. It was Angelo Giuseppe's experience of the world wars that exposed him to people of other faiths, such as non-Catholic Christians, Jews, and Muslims.

In 1889 Angelino was confirmed in the Church of Carvico and then admitted to Holy Communion. Between 1887 and 1890 he received his first education in grade school, and in

1890–91 Fr. Pietro Bolis, parish priest of Carvico, gave him classes in Latin and Italian. He studied in Celana in a school founded by St. Charles Borromeo, the model saint of Catholicism post-Council of Trent, who was canonized in 1610.

In 1892, at age eleven, Angelo Giuseppe entered the seminary (*seminario minore*), and in 1895 the *seminario maggiore*. In 1895 he received the clerical habit, and between 1898 and 1899 the minor orders. For the Roncalli family, sending Angelo Giuseppe to the seminary was possible only through two benefactors who helped pay tuition, the canon Giovanni Morlani and Fr. Francesco Rebuzzini. Roncalli always remembered the financial difficulties of his family without romanticizing poverty and with no sense of shame or guilt. Poverty was a gate for better understanding God in his life—a life that might have been planned differently in a family with more financial resources.

Gaetano Guindani, bishop of Bergamo from 1879 until his death in 1904, was the first bishop Angelo Giuseppe met. Roncalli's aspiration in life was to be a pastor in the church, and Guindani was the first in a series of important episcopal figures in the career of the future John XXIII. Guindani's consecrator in 1873 had been Geremia Bonomelli, bishop of Cremona, one of the most important church leaders in Italian "social Catholicism" at the end of the nineteenth century. In 1893 Guindani published a commentary on Leo XIII's social encyclical *Rerum Novarum* (1891), causing some uproar among the priests of his diocese for the "social views" of their bishop.[2]

2. See Giorgio Vecchio, "I vescovi lombardi e l'enciclica Rerum Novarum," *I tempi della "Rerum Novarum,"* Gabriele de Rosa, ed. (Rome/Soveria Mannelli: Istituto Luigi Sturzo—Rubbettino, 2002), 412.

The first years of Angelo Giuseppe's formation took the form of rules to be scrupulously observed—daily guidelines for the nourishment of the soul and the avoidance of sins and vices to which the young seminarian saw himself inclined. At the end of 1895, at the age of fourteen, he began to write *Il Giornale dell'Anima* (Journal of a Soul), a journal that he kept his entire life. It took different forms—a spiritual journal; entries from retreats and spiritual exercises; and day-by-day notes of appointments, meetings, and remarkable events of the day. The first few years of his spiritual notes included ongoing comments about the poor quality of his Christian character, based on no particular reason but just a fundamental feeling of inadequacy compared to the high standards set by the saints of the Catholic tradition and especially of the Counter-Reformation.

On the first page of *Il Giornale dell'Anima*, Roncalli included part of a canon of the decree of reformation from Session XXII of the Council of Trent. It was about the life of priests and their need to control their lives and customs "in order to conform their dress, gestures, gait, and conversation" to the standards of a life shaped by religion. Roncalli built his life around three foci: "devotion, study, and discipline" and wrote his "rules for life, to be observed by youth willing to be proficient on the way of piety and the studies."[3] They included the following:

- fifteen minutes of "mental prayer" upon waking and one hour of spiritual reading in the evening (from Scripture, St. Philip Neri, St. Francis de Sales, and others) every day;

3. Angelo Giuseppe Roncalli, *Il Giornale dell'Anima*, 24.

- confession and Eucharist every week, with fasting every Friday and Saturday;
- choosing a patron saint and one day of a special retreat every month;
- general confession and spiritual exercises once every year, paying attention to staying away from temptations encountered while on vacation;
- deepening the virtues of charity, purity, chastity, humility, and avoiding improper familiarity of any kind with women "of any condition, age, and degree of relationship."[4]

The seminary young Roncalli attended was separated from the world in order to ensure that the cultural and moral formation of a cleric was different from lay persons outside the seminary. The use of dialect was forbidden; gambling, games, or theater were not allowed; reading of "good literature" was encouraged to avoid the temptations coming from poetry; and spiritual life was punctuated by prayer and devotions. The closest example for young seminarians was St. Aloysius Gonzaga (1568–1591), a model of purity and devotion to the Virgin Mary.[5]

Roncalli found his times of vacation from the seminary particularly full of temptations. In 1895 he wrote "Method of Life for My Vacations," building for himself a very tight schedule of prayer, meditations, study, liturgies, and examinations of conscience—and staying clear of populated

4. Ibid., 4 (spiritual notes for 1895). See also Alberto Melloni, *Papa Giovanni. Un cristiano e il suo concilio* (Turin, Italy: Einaudi, 2009), 49–79.

5. Maurilio Guasco, *Storia del clero in Italia dall'Ottocento a oggi* (Roma/Bari: Laterza, 1997), 64–155.

places and public squares, instead choosing for his walks less populated places.[6]

The rules for the formation of his habits and mentality came from a Jesuitical model, very common to seminary education in the nineteenth century. This would gradually shape the whole structure of *Il Giornale dell'Anima* from 1896 on, when "Ad majorem Dei gloriam" appeared as a recurrent theme in the headings or in the body of the spiritual annotations. The sources for the spiritual and theological formation of Roncalli were Tertullian, Thomas à Kempis, St. John Vianney, Teresa of Ávila, Robert Bellarmine, Francis de Sales, and Francis of Assisi. The most important book for Roncalli was the *Imitatio Christi* by Thomas à Kempis: this was a key source for the *ressourcement* of Roncalli's theology because it allowed him to go back to the sources of the Christian spiritual tradition beyond the "Tridentine paradigm" ruling modern Catholicism until Vatican II.[7]

As a teenager, Roncalli aimed at spiritual perfection with remarkable seriousness. His name called him to be like "an angel": "I am a cleric, therefore I have to be with God like an angel. . . . But what a shame for me, always to be called an angel, to have to behave like an angel, without ever having been really an angel. My name *Angelo* must be for me an encouragement to be really an angel cleric . . . because actually I am far from being an angel."[8]

6. Roncalli, *Il Giornale dell'Anima*, 21–24 (spiritual notes for 1895).

7. Giuseppe Alberigo, *Dalla laguna al Tevere. Angelo Giuseppe Roncalli da San Marco a San Pietro* (Bologna: il Mulino, 2000), 19–20. Roncalli read particularly book III of the *Imitatio*, focused on the themes of peace and grace.

8. Roncalli, *Il Giornale dell'Anima*, 44 (spiritual notes for 1898).

In April 1898, at the end of Holy Week, Roncalli still saw himself far from the ideal model of a priest and of a Christian set by the seminary education. His private journal makes evident a sequence of self-accusations of not being pious enough, humble enough: "The Holy Week has passed, vacations have gone, and I, instead of improving myself, kept going backwards. Is that possible, after all the promises I had made? . . . My Jesus, mercy! I do not know how to explain this."[9] The biggest temptation for Roncalli's moral rectitude was the time of vacation, far from the tight schedule of the seminary and influence of peers and seminary directors. Roncalli knew that sometimes seminary gossip exaggerated minor things, but even in those cases, young Angelo accepted the rebuke as grounded in something he had done wrong, if not in practice, in his heart: "My superiors heard things about me, that I think were exaggerated about the pride I showed during my vacations, and for that I was scolded. I had to humiliate myself without need, but in the end, there is something to that. . . . I have to prepare myself better for those damn holidays" (*maledette vacanze*).[10]

Young Roncalli's life was divided between the seminary in the urban setting of Bergamo and his home village of Sotto il Monte. Attending school sometimes meant walking for much of the day to cover the ten miles from Sotto il Monte to Bergamo.[11] In November 1898, Roncalli returned to the seminary from the summer break and began his theological formation. Slowly his responsibilities in the life of the seminary grew: he became "prefect" (assistant) of one of the classes of the "ginnasio" (ninth grade). But that did

9. Ibid., 49 (April 22, 1898).
10. Ibid., 53 (June 5, 1898).
11. Ibid., 86 (November 3, 1898).

not improve Roncalli's opinion of himself or his perception that others thought of him as naïve and gullible. He took this as one more reason to work on his humility: "I only have reasons to rejoice [of my reputation as a naïve and gullible person] because this way my pride gets even more humiliated—not unlike, although in a very distant and unworthy way, the treatment Jesus received."[12]

The year 1900 was a year of jubilee, a "holy year" for the Catholic Church. In September, nineteen-year-old Angelo Giuseppe traveled to Rome, Loreto, and Assisi on a pilgrimage. (He repeated the same itinerary sixty-two years later, a few days before the opening of Vatican II.) A few months before his pilgrimage, he made a solemn promise to the Sacred Heart of Jesus under the auspices of St. Aloysius Gonzaga: "I promise, with solemnity and strength, that this act can keep myself pure, today and forever, from any attachment to any voluntary venial sin, thanks to God's grace."[13] Later that year Roncalli recorded in his journal the "rules" of St. Francis de Sales and put them in practice at the age of twenty while studying law at the University of Padua: "against pride, for a more orderly way to interact with other persons; modesty and civility without being austere and melancholic; friend of all and intimate with few; discretion." Roncalli described a different attitude toward sin and the failure to be at the level of ideal standards: "With those sad and melancholic people, who like to show their flaws, I'll be watchful and I will say nothing, because these people would be able to talk for ten years and more even on the slightest imperfection. And then, what purpose is

12. Ibid., 92 (April 16, 1899).
13. Ibid., 109 (February 27, 1900).

served by the disclosure of the faults we commit? Are they
not visible enough? Do not they show by themselves?"[14]

A Lombard Studying in Rome (1901–1904)

Early in the morning on January 4, 1901, Angelo Giuseppe Roncalli arrived in Rome to continue his seminary
formation. He lived in the Seminario Romano, thanks to a
scholarship from the Fondazione Canonico Flaminio Cera-
sola, a Catholic foundation from Bergamo that ran a college
in Rome connected with the Seminario Romano. Two other
seminarians from Bergamo went to Rome with him. Roncalli was chosen as the best among the brightest seminarians
from Bergamo. He stayed in Rome until the end of 1904,
except from the end of 1901 until the end of 1902 because
of his military service in Bergamo, which was an experience
that opened his eyes to the world outside of the seminary.[15]

Roncalli studied theology at the Seminario Romano, not
a field considered "high profile" from an academic standpoint, but nevertheless representing a wave of new cultural
inputs for the young student from a small village. During
this time Roncalli experienced Rome as the capital of Italy
and the Rome of the Catholic Church. He had been in Rome
only once, the year before in September 1900, for a diocesan
pilgrimage. At the time, Rome was still considered the capital
of a nation that according to the reactionary Catholic propaganda "robbed" the papacy of the Papal States. Church
and Italy were far from reconciled; they coexisted in a relationship marked by cautious and undeclared cultural and

14. Ibid., 110 (spiritual notes for 1900).
15. Until the year 1929 there was no concordat between Italy and
the Holy See, and therefore seminarians had to serve in the military.

political negotiation. The nationalist sentiments of the new Italy and the bitter resentment of many bishops and priests required adjustments after centuries of a "nationless" Italy dominated by the popes and foreign powers.

Rome changed Angelo Giuseppe's daily routine, and his spiritual and intellectual life evolved. By April 1901 he felt that Rome was also about "acquiring good scholarship, in order to earn souls for Christ through this route that has now become most important."[16] Roncalli received his degree in theology in June 1901, during the time when Rome was part of the beginning of a new relationship between theology and science—one that Leo XIII had criticized in 1902 and was harshly repressed by Pius X in the antimodernist purge in 1907. Roncalli was in touch with those intellectuals and teachers, but as a student it was from a distance.[17] When John XXIII was elected pope in 1958, some tried to paint him with the heretical "modernist" brush by recirculating critiques of modernism from 1907–8, but to no avail. Although these accusations may have damaged his career as a young scholar and priest working in Catholic institutions in Rome, they would not have that same effect on him decades later.

The visible change in Angelo Giuseppe's approach to his spiritual life happened when he first met with the spiritual director of Seminario Romano, the Liguorian Francesco Pitocchi (1852–1922). He wrote, "December 19, 1902: *God is everything: I am nothing.* And that is all for today."[18] That counterpoint to Teresa of Ávila's famous "*solo Dios basta*"

16. Roncalli, *Il Giornale dell'Anima*, 126 (April 28, 1901).

17. Peter Hebblethwaite, *John XXIII. Pope of the Century* (London/New York: Continuum, 1984), 20.

18. Roncalli, *Il Giornale dell'Anima*, 141 (December 16, 1902).

(in Italian he wrote instead "e per oggi basta") marked the end of the spiritual hyper-perfectionism typical of the early years of Roncalli in the seminary in Bergamo. Almost paradoxically, the usual perception of Rome as guilt-inducing for Catholics was for Roncalli the beginning of a journey toward a more reconciled view of himself and his moral life in relation to God. A few days later he wrote, "In me God is everything and I am nothing. I am a sinner and much more miserable than I can imagine. If I had done something good in my life it was all the work of God, that would produce the best results if I had not hindered and prevented. . . . The rule must be the object of all my care, not only the rule in general, but each and every rule in particular. . . . *I should not want to be what I am not, but I should be very good at what I am*—so says my St. Francis de Sales."[19]

In Rome, Roncalli began not only his theological studies but also the development of his spiritual life: "I will start again as if thus far I had done nothing, nothing."[20] This was the beginning of a key idea for Roncalli, later John XXIII: renewal as *aggiornamento*—"the past is no longer an oppressive mortgage on our today."[21] For Roncalli this was a critical reexamination of his past spiritual practices: "I am convinced the idea of sainthood that I applied to myself was false. I always asked myself, 'In this instance, what would St. Louis do and not do, or would he do this or that?' I could never achieve what I had imagined I could do, and I became anxious. It is a wrong system. From the virtues of the saints

19. Ibid., 144–45 (December 20, 1902; emphasis mine).
20. Ibid., 162 (January 19, 1903).
21. Alberto Melloni, *Il "Giornale dell'anima" di Giovanni XXIII* (Milan, Italy: Jaca Book, 2000), 88.

I must take the substance and not the details."[22] Roncalli began to reject a "one-size-fits-all" idea of sainthood.

The difference between the substance and the details (*la sostanza e gli accidenti*) became crucial in Roncalli's understanding of the nature of his spiritual life and also of the life of the church in general. The same thing happened in his intellectual approach to theology and the beginning of his interest in history. His professor of church history, Umberto Benigni (who later, from 1907 on, became the most inflexible of the antimodernist persecutors during the pontificate of Pius X) told students: "Do not read much, but read well." Roncalli was part of that Catholic world that, even in the closely watched institutions of higher education for church officials in Rome, received important intellectual contributions from eminent academics (such as Louis Duchesne and Henri Denifle), representatives of the incipient historical-critical approach to Catholic theology and church history.[23] Those were the very same years—immediately after the condemnation of theological Americanism by Leo XIII in 1899—when Italian Catholicism was looking with curiosity at American Catholicism and at important episcopal figures in the United States, including James Gibbons, John Ireland, and John Lancaster Spalding (who delivered an important lecture in Rome in the spring of 1900 on education and cultural renewal in the church).[24] Roncalli would have liked

22. Roncalli, *Il Giornale dell'Anima*, 159–60 (January 16, 1903).

23. Stefano Trinchese, *Roncalli "storico." L'interesse per la storia nella formazione e negli studi di papa Giovanni XXIII (1905–1958)* (Chieti, Italy: Solfanelli, 1988).

24. Daniela Saresella, *Cattolicesimo italiano e sfida americana* (Brescia: Morcelliana, 2001); Ornella Confessore, *L'americanismo cattolico in Italia* (Rome: Studium, 1984).

to have the opportunity to go deeper in his studies, but his superiors at the Seminario Romano "did not allow that."[25] Nevertheless, Roncalli studied Spalding with particular interest.[26]

Young Angelo Giuseppe witnessed church history happening in Rome on February 20, 1903, when the church celebrated the twenty-fifth anniversary of the pontificate of Leo XIII (then ninety-three years old). The seminarian from Bergamo went to St. Peter's Square and celebrated the event with poetic words about the Holy Father, but at the same time looked to a future when friends and enemies of the church "would embrace as brothers in front of the throne not of a sovereign but of a Father."[27] It was an annoucement of Roncalli's interpretation of episcopal ministry: being a father. It also applied to the bishop of Rome who had been deprived of his temporal power only a few years before.

For the young Catholic Roncalli, Rome was really the center of the world. Between the twenty-fifth anniversary of Leo XIII and the death of the pope on July 20, 1903, Roncalli saw visits to the Vatican by Edward VII, king and emperor of the United Kingdom (who was on his way to India) and the visit of Wilhelm II, emperor of Germany. In August 1903, Pius X was elected by the conclave; Roncalli had seen him celebrate Mass in Bergamo in August 1898. It was the beginning of a difficult period for the church with theologians and scholars repressed by the institution for their historical-critical approach to theology. Roncalli was

25. Roncalli, *Il Giornale dell'Anima*, 132 (December 1902).

26. Lucia Butturini, "Tradizione e rinnovamento nelle riflessioni del giovane Roncalli," in *Un cristiano sul trono di Pietro. Studi storici su Giovanni XXIII*, Fondazione per le scienze religiose di Bologna, ed. (Gorle, Italy: Servitium, 2003) 13–70.

27. Roncalli, *Il Giornale dell'Anima*, 169.

aware of that, and tried to mediate between his intellectual curiosity and his solid formation:

> I will always investigate the sacred sciences. In matters theological or biblical, I will investigate first the traditional doctrine of the church, and based on that, I will judge the latest science. I do not disregard the critical approach, and I will stay away from thinking ominously or disrespectfully of the critical approach. I indeed love the critical studies: I will follow with passion the latest results of its investigations; I will make myself aware of new systems in its incessant developments; I will study its trends. Critical approach is for me light and truth, and the truth is holy and one. However I will endeavor always to bring to these discussions a great moderation, harmony, balance, and serenity of judgment, not separated by a prudent and circumspect mindedness. In points that are in doubt, I will choose to be silent as if I were ignorant instead of venturing into propositions differing from the right thinking of the church. I will never be surprised about anything, although certain conclusions, though still intact in the sacred deposit of faith, were to be a little surprising. Surprise is the daughter of ignorance mostly. In fact I will take consolation from the fact that God has prepared everything to make more clear and more pure the sacred treasure of his revelation. In general my rule will be to listen to everything and everyone, thinking and studying much, and being slow to judge: do not gossip, do not make noise, and keep an eye on the thinking of the church without ever moving an iota of distance from her.[28]

Although surrounded by the clerical culture of Italian Catholicism between the end of the nineteenth and beginning

---

28. Ibid., 211–12 (December 9–18, 1903).

of the twentieth centuries—what historian of clerical culture Maurilio Guasco called "a spirituality of submission"[29]— Roncalli was already looking at the role of critical knowledge in its relationship to the tradition of the church as a key element to his pastoral call. In December 1903, Roncalli received the ordination to deacon, and on August 10, 1904, he became a priest. In his notes during his retreat to prepare for ordination, Roncalli wondered what he would become: "What will become of me in the future? Will I become a good theologian, a jurist, a country priest, a bishop, a cardinal, a diplomat, a pope, or a simple poor priest? Should that all matter to me? I must be none of this and even more than that, following the divine provisions. My God is everything: *Deus meus est omnia.* The good Jesus will send up in smoke my ideals of ambition and reputation before the world."[30]

The beginning of Roncalli's life as a priest coincided with a delicate moment in the history of Italian Catholicism. In July 1904 Roncalli received his doctorate in theology. The proctor for his written exam was Eugenio Pacelli, future Pius XII; the one who would make him cardinal fifty years later, would be his predecessor on the chair of Peter. A few weeks later, in August 1904, he was ordained priest in the Church of Santa Maria in Monte Santo, in Piazza del Popolo in Rome. But 1904 was important for Italian Catholicism for other reasons, too. The Vatican put an end to the important experiences of "social action" of Italian lay Catholics organized in the "Opera dei Congressi"—an active and effective organization especially in the part of Italy from where Roncalli came. The year 1904 meant the beginning of more strict control by the Vatican on the initiatives of

29. Guasco, *Storia del clero in Italia*, 152–55.
30. Roncalli, *Il Giornale dell'Anima*, 227 (August 1–10, 1904).

Italian Catholics, especially related to social and political action. This would have an impact on Roncalli in the next few years in his role as secretary of the new bishop of Bergamo. The new pontificate of Pius X meant a significant restriction in the academic freedom of theologians, seminarians, clergy, and laity. The period was marked by the antimodernist "purge" inaugurated by the "syllabus" of 1907, the letter *Lamentabili*, which was expanded a couple of months later (September 1907) by the encyclical *Pascendi Dominici Gregis.*[31]

31. Claus Arnold and Giovanni Vian, eds. *La condanna del modernismo: documenti, interpretazioni, conseguenze* (Rome: Viella, 2010); Guido Verucci, *L'eresia del Novecento: la Chiesa e la repressione del modernismo in Italia* (Turin, Italy: Einaudi, 2010).

CHAPTER TWO

Dangerous Times: Antimodernism, World War, and Curia Politics

(1905–1924)

Secretary of Bishop Radini Tedeschi (1905–1914)

On January 8, 1905, Giacomo Maria Radini Tedeschi was appointed bishop of Bergamo. Radini was one of the most important bishops of pre-World War I Italian Catholicism, and for Roncalli, who was appointed his secretary a few days later, this was a transformative experience as a priest and as an intellectual.[1] Radini was engaged with the social aspect of Italian Catholicism, convinced of the need of a "pastoral modernity" in the church, and was part of a large network of notable bishops and theologians in Italy and in Europe. Radini called a synod for his diocese, gave his moral and

---

1. Mario Benigni, *Papa Giovanni XXIII chierico e sacerdote a Bergamo 1892–1921* (Milan, Italy: Glossa, 1998); Giuseppe Battelli, *Un pastore tra fede e ideologia. Giacomo Maria Radini Tedeschi 1857–1914* (Genoa: Marietti, 1988).

financial support to the workers on strike at the cotton factory in Ranica (the strike lasted fifty days), and sent some of his priests to study in Jerusalem and in Leuven, Belgium, one of the most important centers of the liturgical movement at the beginning of the twentieth century.

For Roncalli, Radini was an example of how to be a bishop for the people and, at the same time, maintain a posture of episcopal dignity and manners based on the guidelines and *ethos* of the bishops of Tridentine Catholicism. Radini was a member of the Italian elite who became a bishop, and came from a background very different from the humble milieu of peasants of the Roncalli family. Life became very busy for Roncalli; he did not have time to write his spiritual journal between 1904 and 1907, and he was worried about being overwhelmed by the flurry of activities and keeping up with his energetic bishop.

Roncalli learned much from Radini because he included his secretary in all the activities of being the bishop of Bergamo. Much of what Radini did at the beginning of his episcopal ministry for the renewal of Christian life in Bergamo, Roncalli later did as a patriarch of Venice, as bishop of Rome, and as pope.[2]

A crucial experience for Roncalli was pastoral visitation, one of the most important tools for the government of the church in the Tridentine period. From December 1905 through the end of 1906, Roncalli accompanied Radini on visits to the 350 parishes of the diocese and kept a detailed record of the conditions of the church buildings and rectories, and of the priests. Roncalli was a keen observer, especially of the liturgical furnishings and objects in the parishes.

2. Giuseppe Alberigo, *Papa Giovanni 1881–1963* (Bologna, Italy: EDB, 2000), 40.

For him, Catholic reform was first of all the reform according to the Council of Trent—not as a church "police" operation, but as pastoral work: "What is the 'pastoral visit'? It is the friend who goes to the friend, the doctor to the infirm, the master to the disciple, the captain to the soldiers, the shepherd to the flock, the father to the children. The bishop is all this, and here is the concept of the pastoral visit."[3]

The fundamental discovery for Roncalli was the pastoral model not only *in* Radini, but especially *through* Radini. It included the pastoral visits in the diocese, but also the spirituality of the Council of Trent and the great episcopal figures of North Italian Catholicism of the immediate post-Trent period such as Charles Borromeo (1538–1584, bishop of Milan) and Gregorio Barbarigo (1625–1697, bishop of Bergamo and then of Padua) as well as the cardinal archbishop of Milan during Roncalli's life, Andrea Carlo Ferrari (1850–1921). But the Tridentine culture of Roncalli was not the Tridentinism stuck in the antimodern posture of what John O'Malley (following British historian Eric Hobsbawm) has called "the long nineteenth century."[4] It was Catholic reform that did not embrace liberal culture, but nevertheless emphasized local bishops dealing with pastoral and social issues—an awareness of the need of a certain pastoral modernity.

Roncalli encountered this social and economic modernity by experiencing firsthand conciliar and collegial dimensions

3. *Diaries 1905–1925*, 20 (December 8, 1905).

4. John W. O'Malley, *What Happened at Vatican II* (Cambridge, MA: Belknap Press of Harvard University Press, 2008); and John W. O'Malley, *Trent. What Happened at the Council* (Cambridge, MA: Belknap Press of Harvard University Press, 2013).

of Italian Catholicism. Several times in 1906 he traveled with Radini to Milan for the meetings of the preparatory commission for the Eighth Provincial Council of the bishops of Lombardia region. That year Roncalli also discovered the original papers of Charles Borromeo regarding the official reports made during his pastoral visit to the diocese of Bergamo.[5] This was the beginning of lengthy historical research that Roncalli pursued his whole life (his last volume was published in 1959).[6] Charles Borromeo became a real focus for Roncalli's historical and theological interests partly because 1910 marked the three-century anniversary of the canonization of one of the symbols of the church of the Council of Trent (Borromeo), and because Roncalli was a member of the diocesan commission for the celebrations of the anniversary of Borromeo's canonization.[7] Borromeo was a model for Roncalli (just as Radini in Bergamo and Ferrari in Milan) of pastoral dynamism and creativity in a church that in the early twentieth century was clearly suffering the antimodernist campaign. In this sense, Roncalli was a "Milanese" or "Lombard" priest more than a "Roman" or "Vatican" priest.

Borromeo was not the only source for the intellectual and theological growth of Roncalli. Roncalli taught a course in church history at the diocesan seminary in 1906; for the course preparation he used *Histoire ancienne de l'Église* by

5. Alberto Melloni, "Il modello di San Carlo Borromeo negli studi e nell'esperienza di Angelo Giuseppe Roncalli," *Rivista di Storia e Letteratura Religiosa* 23 (1987), 68–114.

6. See Angelo Giuseppe Roncalli, *Gli Atti della Visita Apostolica di S. Carlo Borromeo a Bergamo (1575)*, with Fr. Pietro Forno, 2 volumes in 5 tomes (Florence, Italy: Olschki, 1936–1958 [but 1936–1959]).

7. Angelo Giuseppe Roncalli, *Il Giornale dell'Anima*, 256 (spiritual notes, September 1909).

Louis Duchesne, an author accused of modernism in 1910–1911. This choice caused accusations of modernism against Roncalli until 1914.[8] Roncalli also read Duchesne on the history of the Christian churches separated from Rome (*Églises séparées*, with a focus on eastern Christianity) and on the history of the liturgy (*Les origines du culte chrétien: étude sur la liturgie latine avant Charlemagne*).[9]

Between 1906 and 1914 Roncalli taught church history in the seminary of Bergamo. He expanded his horizons by traveling, especially with a pilgrimage to the Holy Land between September and November of 1906. He learned about the vast world from the variety of people on the ship from Italy to Beirut: "We are more than a hundred of all social classes: the archbishop of Los Angeles (who has the pastoral care of two million souls), a prince, a knight, a poor seller of devotional books from a parish in Lodi, a poor woman from our countryside looked forward to returning to her family to recount the wonders of the land of Jesus."[10] Roncalli saw the decay of the Ottoman Empire. While in Jaffa he wrote, "The muezzins call to prayer from their minarets. . . . We pray to the Lord that he welcomes

8. Louis Duchesne, *Histoire ancienne de l'Église* (Paris: Albert Fon[te]moing, 1906). See Lucia Butturini, "Roncalli tra Roma e Bergamo (1901–1920): esperienze, letture, riflessioni," *Rivisitare Giovanni XXIII* ("Cristianesimo nella Storia," XXV/2), Enrico Galavotti, ed. (Bologna, Italy: Dehoniane, 2004), 353–86; Stefano Trinchese, "A.G. Roncalli e i sospetti di modernismo," in *Il modernismo tra cristianità e secolarizzazione*, Alfondo Botti and Rocco Cerrato, eds., (Urbino, Italy: Quattroventi, 2001), 727–70.

9. Louis Duchesne, *Églises séparées* (Paris: Albert Fontemoing 1896); Louis Duchesne, *Les origines du culte chrétien: étude sur la liturgie latine avant Charlemagne* (Paris: Albert Fontemoing, 1902).

10. *Diaries 1905–1925*, 148 (September 24, 1906).

everyone in his mercy, sweeping the East from this Muslim government that hangs over these people like a dark shadow of injustice and unprecedented barbarity."[11]

Serving as the secretary of the bishop and teaching in the seminary brought Roncalli back to the life he liked. "I have come back to the life of a seminarian, and I want to live my life like a seminarian."[12] But he was also aware of the delicacy of the work of bishop's secretary. "My job as a secretary of the bishop imposes on me serious concerns and delicate duties. . . . I will never forget what Pope Pius X told me when I came to Bergamo with Bishop [Radini]: 'So, Fr. Angelo, *fidelis servus prudens . . . et prudens.*' About the remarks made by the world, *laetari et benefacere*, and let the sparrows sing."[13]

In the fall of 1907 Roncalli had time to do pastoral work in a parish a few miles from Bergamo, in Sforzatica Santa Maria. At the same time, the twenty-six-year-old Roncalli prepared his first scholarly paper, which he presented on December 4, 1907. It was about the church historian Cesare Baronio (1538–1607), author of the famous work of church history *Annales Ecclesiastici.* He began writing for the local newspaper *L'Eco di Bergamo* and for the new monthly of the diocese, *La Vita Diocesana* (inspired by the monthly created by Cardinal Mercier for the diocese of Malines, Belgium). He also began his research on the pastoral visit of Borromeo in Bergamo.[14] Thanks to the connections of his bishop, Roncalli had the opportunity to meet important

11. Ibid., 168 (October 4, 1906).

12. Roncalli, *Il Giornale dell'Anima*, 245–46 (spiritual notes, September 1907).

13. Ibid., 248 (spiritual notes, September 1907).

14. See Alberto Melloni, *Papa Giovanni. Un cristiano e il suo concilio* (Turin, Italy: Einaudi, 2009), 61.

church leaders of his time, such as cardinals Antonio Ferrari (Milan), Désiré Mercier (Malines, Belgium), Pietro Maffi (Pisa), and Bishop Geremia Bonomelli. He also met leaders of the lay Catholic movement in Italy, such as Giovanni Grosoli, Giuseppe Toniolo, and Giuseppe Dalla Torre. These contacts acquainted him with the social concerns in his own diocese, especially the plight of workers employed by the local cotton mill in the famous fifty-day strike that began on September 22, 1909. Both Radini and Roncalli supported the strike and contributed their own money to help the striking workers. When this news arrived in Rome, the Vatican establishment was concerned about these concrete manifestations of social Catholicism from the bishop and his secretary.

At that time, the diocese of Bergamo and Bishop Radini were already dangerously close to the attention of the Vatican of Pius X. In June and August 1908, the diocese received two apostolic visitations—Pius X's tool of choice for the correction of "modernist errors" in local churches and seminaries. One year later, in August 1909, the bishop of Bergamo was informed of the criticisms by the Rome-appointed visitor, Msgr. Andrea Sarti (bishop of Guastalla) against the situation of the diocese in a long letter from the Concistorial Congregation of the Roman Curia. The criticisms included modernist priests, excessive indulgence for the workers unions, too much activity of lay Catholic organizations, and an intellectual environment not careful enough about the dangers for theology coming from modern social and human sciences. In November 1909, Pope Pius X personally wrote a letter to the bishop of Bergamo asking explanations about a catechism published by a priest of the diocese.[15] This attention from the Vatican

15. *Diaries 1905–1925*, introduction by Lucia Butturini, 13–15.

put the diocese, including Roncalli because of his relationship with his bishop, in a situation of ongoing tension with Rome because of a lack of trust. This exposed Roncalli to a particularly difficult situation, given that from the beginning of 1909 he acted as a *de facto* editor of the diocesan paper. Roncalli was aware of the dangers of the situation and in 1910 wrote in his spiritual journal:

> It pleased Blessed Jesus to give me in these spiritual exercises a light to understand even more strongly the need to keep intact and pure my *sensus fidei* and my *sentire cum ecclesia,* and it made me see in a most gorgeous light the wisdom, the opportunity, and the beauty of the measures decided by the papal authority designed to protect people, especially the clergy, from the infection of modern errors (so-called modernism). . . . Several people, even good ones, have fallen into this ambiguity, perhaps unconsciously, and they were led on the fields of the error. . . .On my knees, I thank the Lord for keeping me unharmed in the midst of such a cauldron and agitation of thoughts and words. . . . I have to remember that the church contains in herself the eternal youth of the truth and of Christ that is of all times; but it is the church that transforms and saves the people and the times, not the other way around.[16]

Roncalli continued to be a faithful member of the church, but at the same time was conscious of the need for the church to be aware of modern times and represent an "integral anthropology, far from privileges and exclusions . . . looking for a composition between faith and history."[17] What was remarkable about Roncalli and typical of his

---

16. Roncalli, *Il Giornale dell'Anima,* 257–59 (September 1910).
17. Alberigo, *Papa Giovanni,* 42.

entire spiritual and intellectual life was his ability to make "choices inspired by wisdom, rather than by a cultural project marked by strong-minded planning and driven by particular milieus or groups."[18]

Roncalli's responsibilities grew. He was appointed vice-secretary of the thirty-third diocesan synod that the diocese of Bergamo celebrated April 26–28, 1910. In July–August 1911 he traveled with Bishop Radini to Switzerland and Austria. It was a crucial moment of Pius X's pontificate when many key players in the church thought that there would soon be a conclave[19] for important meetings of church leaders. Roncalli met Cardinal Mariano Rampolla who was then secretary of the Holy Office and the last one to be denied, in the conclave of 1903, the election to the chair of Peter by the right of *veto* of the Austrian emperor. He also met professors of the University of Fribourg. In September 1912 Radini sent Roncalli to the international eucharistic congress in Vienna and he took the opportunity to visit Munich, Salzburg, Krakow, and Budapest. Roncalli would later spend almost twenty years of his life in eastern Europe.

Roncalli's worldview was marked by a sense of geography but even more by history. In 1912 he was asked as a church historian to draft the document of the bishops of the Lombardia region about the 1,600 years of the "Edict of Milan," which was published by Roman emperor Constantine and was a landmark document giving religious liberty to Christians in the Roman Empire (313–1913).[20] His ministry in the

18. *Diaries 1905–1925*, introduction by Lucia Butturini, xxiii.
19. About the so-called "pre-conclave meeting of Einsiedeln" of the fall of 1911, see *Il Giornale dell'Anima*, 265–66 (October 1912).
20. The collective letter of the bishops from Lombardia is published in *Vita Diocesana* 4 (1912); 299–334. About the historical

diocese was also marked by contacts with early advocates of action by women in the Catholic Church. He had to moderate and direct groups of lay activists, sometimes marked by internecine fights: "My ministry is very delicate and dangerous, given that I have to deal often with women. I propose therefore to always maintain an attitude of goodness, modesty, and seriousness that will make me forget my person and will make my work spiritually effective."[21] In November 1912 Roncalli continued his spiritual journey by joining a congregation of diocesan priests, the "Priests of the Sacred Heart." "My decision requires nothing more from me than what I already promised the Lord, that is, to keep myself at the disposal of my superiors, without doing anything that can move them in one direction or another for what concerns me."[22]

The War and Pastoral Care of the Youth (1914–1920)

The death of Pius X on August 20, 1914, was followed two days later by the untimely death of Bishop Radini Tedeschi, which meant a radical change in Roncalli's life. Without tasks delegated by the bishop, Roncalli served as a priest. It became a difficult time for him given the tensions between clergy and laity within the diocese in Bergamo during the years of Radini Tedeschi and the accusations coming from Rome via local informants who were not pleased with his pastoral style and sociocultural leanings. It was not surprising later that year when "the first bitter experiences of

works of Roncalli see Angelo Giuseppe Roncalli. *Chierico e storico a Bergamo. Antologia di scritti (1907–1912)*, Francesco Mores, ed. (Rome: Edizioni di Storia e Letteratura, 2008).

21. Roncalli, *Il Giornale dell'Anima*, 265 (October 1912).
22. Ibid., 255 (September 1909).

Roncalli with the Roman Curia" occurred.[23] A few weeks before his death, Radini had an audience in the Vatican with Cardinal Gaetano De Lai, the secretary of the Consistorial Congregation of the Roman Curia, who accused him, based on rumors from Bergamo, of a lack of dogmatic rigor in his teaching activity. But even in those difficult circumstances Roncalli tried not to change his interior disposition. In the reflections for the tenth anniversary of his ordination in 1914 (just before Radini's death), he had written:

> The particular attitudes of my character, my experiences, and my circumstances lead me to work quietly and peacefully outside of the battlefield, rather than in a pugnacious manner as in a controversy or fight. I do not want to become a saint disfiguring the decent original I am and to become an unhappy copy of others who have a nature that is markedly different from mine. But this spirit of peace should not be acquiescence to self-love, to satisfaction of myself, or to acquiescence of thought, principles, and attitudes. The usual smile that touches the lip must be able to conceal the internal struggle—sometimes tremendous—against selfishness, and must represent the victories of the spirit over the contractions of the sense and of self-love. . . . I will let other people pass over me; I will stay where Providence puts me, clearing the way for others. I want to keep my peace, which is my freedom.[24]

When Radini died, Roncalli left the episcopal chancery and moved to the seminary, waiting for the appointment of the new bishop. Returning to the seminary where he was a professor meant he began a new life while, at the same time,

23. Alberigo, *Papa Giovanni*, 48.
24. Roncalli, *Il Giornale dell'Anima*, 271–72 (August 10, 1914).

keeping up his old life: "My new position will give the whole of me to the seminary, even if I will not leave the ministry of souls. Mine will be a life of greater peace and greater reflection, just as I wished. This is a new grace that the Lord gives me."[25]

In his journal during those days of change, Roncalli promised obedience to the new bishop (whoever he would be), but reminded himself that other material changes were going to happen in his life. "I will be vigilant to keep myself distant from every concern about my future. I was born poor, and I will die poor, sure that at the proper hour the Divine Providence will not leave me without the necessary, giving me even the convenient and the abundant."[26]

These weeks of transition for Roncalli coincided with a more general time of change: World War I began, Pius X died, and a new pope, Benedict XV, was elected. The war did not involve Italy until April 1915 and in May 1915 Fr. Angelo was called to serve once again as a military chaplain, which he did until 1918. He had served already in peace time 1901–1902. The day before Italy entered the war he wrote, "Tomorrow I leave for military service in the health services. Where will they send me? To the enemy front? Will I be back in Bergamo or has the Lord prepared me for my last hour on the field of war? I know nothing, only that I always want the will of God in everything and his glory in the complete sacrifice of my being. This is I think the only way to keep myself true to my vocation and to show my true love for the motherland and for the souls of my brothers."[27] During the war he served at the military

25. Ibid., 275 (September 1914).
26. Ibid., 277 (September 1914).
27. Ibid., 279 (May 23, 1915).

hospital in Bergamo as a reserve sergeant; he wrote often to his family, and especially to his brother Saverio who was also serving in the military. At the beginning of 1917 Roncalli wondered if he was going to be sent to face the enemy instead of tending wounded and dying soldiers in the hospital. In a letter to his brother he wrote, "Today I had a medical examination and I have been declared *fit for war service*. I wonder if they will send me too to the front. If they do, I shall go willingly because I hope to be able to do a little good there, too."[28]

For Roncalli, as well as for the Italian clergy and the Italian Catholic Church, World War I was a key experience in the shaping of a sense of national unity. It was the biggest bloodbath in Italian history up to that moment, and the Catholic Church, despite the grievances of the papacy against the "liberals" governing Italy, joined in the patriotic effort.[29] Roncalli was not a pacifist, but clearly rejected the rhetoric of war and was not absorbed (as many other priests were in this period) in the nationalist-religious propaganda for the war. This experience would be visible almost fifty years later with his encyclical *Pacem in Terris*, published a few weeks before his death in 1963.

During the war Roncalli continued his intellectual work; for a period of time he taught in the seminary of Bergamo and in 1916 published a biography of bishop Radini Tedeschi.[30] Father Roncalli was also at the hospital in contact

28. *Pope John XXIII, Letters to His Family*, trans. Dorothy White (New York/Toronto: McGraw Hill, 1970), 33.

29. See Roberto Morozzo della Rocca, *La fede e la guerra. Cappellani militari e preti soldati (1915–1919)* (Rome: Studium, 1980).

30. See Angelo Giuseppe Roncalli, *In memoria di Mons. Giacomo Maria Radini Tedeschi vescovo di Bergamo* (Bergamo, Italy:

with young soldiers dying every day and with a variety of persons coming from different social and religious backgrounds. He decided not to infringe on the conscience of a freemason woman, and he respected the "good faith" of a non-Catholic Christian (a lieutenant and member of the Waldensian Evangelical Church). Roncalli prayed for a Muslim soldier, having trust that "the Lord will save him."[31] The soldier was baptized *sub condicione* by a nun in the hospital, and when the Muslim soldier died, Roncalli decided not to tell the mufti who buried him.

Roncalli's situation was different from many of the other priests in his diocese and in the seminary: "These good priests live sitting on their academic chairs and among books, and they look at the war from afar. It is my duty instead, and it is a blessing for me, to stay in touch with the souls, and be involved in a daily experience that is certainly greater and more poignant than their experience."[32]

These pastoral and human experiences opened his eyes to world politics and to a complex sense of national identity for an Italian Catholic. Roncalli expressed his "love for Italy, but hatred for the governments that have run it thus far."[33] His sarcastic judgment on Italian military elites was clear when he reported what German soldiers said about Italians: "'Soldiers of iron; guns of wood; officers of paper.' It is

---

Sant'Alessandro, 1916); second edition (Rome: Edizioni di Storia e Letteratura,1963); *My bishop. A portrait of Msgr. Giacomo Maria Radini Tedeschi*, English trans. with foreword by H.E. Cardinale and introduction by Loris Capovilla, trans. Dorothy White (New York: McGraw-Hill, 1969).

31. *Diaries 1905–1925*, 314 (March 31, 1918), 321 (May 1, 1918), and 368–71 (October 5 and 10, 1918).

32. Ibid., 324 (May 16, 1918).

33. Ibid., 296 (January 31, 1918).

probably a tale, but it says a lot."[34] In the enthusiasm of the days of victory in November 1918, he also had harsh words for the Germany of Martin Luther: "The fall of Germany with the breakup of its idols is truly impressive. For me it is Luther that receives a powerful blow in his thinking, in his spirit."[35] This anti-Lutheranism was typical of nineteenth-century Catholic culture. But it was for the kaiser of Germany, Wilhelm II, that Roncalli leveled his strongest criticism: "Here you have a man who said always *Domine, Domine*, but he dealt with the Lord just like with a fellow of his. For sure he did not do the Lord's work."[36] Regarding Italy, Roncalli despised "freemasonic liberalism" and saw Italy's future shaped by two political forces: Catholics and socialists.[37] He was not involved in politics personally, but as a historian he possessed a solid political perception.

The end of the war was a period of transition for Europe as well as for Roncalli. The thirty-eight-year-old priest was changed by what he had seen and by the people he had met, and his sense of apostolic mission was renewed by what he had seen of the world. He did not blame "the world" (metaphysically understood) for being against the church, as was typical for an official Catholic culture still reproaching the world for the rejection of the high sovereignty of Catholicism on the world. Roncalli understood in a deeper way the future of his pastoral calling:

> In these four years of war that passed in the midst of a world in convulsions, the Lord sent many blessings to me:

34. Ibid., 299 (February 1, 1918).
35. Ibid., 377 (November 12, 1918).
36. Ibid., 375 (November 9, 1918).
37. Ibid., 292 (December 1, 1917).

how much experience, how many opportunities to do good to my brothers! My Jesus, I thank you and bless you. I remember the many souls of young people I approached at this time, many of whom I accompanied to the other life, and I still feel moved by the thought they will pray for me, which gives me comfort and encouragement. When I awake in the light of a new day, I remember the highest principles of faith and of a Christian and priestly life that were by the grace of God the food of my youth: the glory of the Lord, my sanctification, heaven, the church, the souls. My contact with the world turns all these principles and lifts them up and turns them into a stronger apostolate.[38]

Roncalli's perception of the social and political situation of Italy grew during the war and was important in light of the new task that Bishop Marelli (Radini's successor) gave him in February of 1918—the pastoral care of the "students' house" in Bergamo, a formational and educational experience for the youth of the diocese that attended public schools. These youth came from a different background than the ones Roncalli had taught in the seminary, where he would later become spiritual director in September of 1919.

During October and November of 1919 Roncalli was in Rome for a few days to attend a conference of the newly created "Union of Catholic Women in Italy" (*Unione Cattolica Femminile Italiana*). He no longer felt comfortable in the city he had left for Bergamo almost fifteen years before, when he left the Seminario Romano: "The benevolence that I received from the people I met in Rome was very dear to me, and it was good for the soul. I must, however, confess that the more I go on in life, the less I feel attached to the Roman milieu. I am comfortable there as a pilgrim, but now

38. Roncalli, *Il Giornale dell'Anima*, 281 (April 28–May 3, 1919).

I would not want to live there permanently, even if I see an immense good that needs to be done."[39] He did not know that he would be back in Rome very soon with a new position close to the Roman Curia.

In Rome for Propaganda Fide (1920–1924)

> Today, Msgr. bishop called and read me a letter written to him by Cardinal Van Rossum, Prefect of Propaganda Fide, in which he requested my bishop to give me to Rome as head of the Directorate General of the Society for the Propagation of the Faith in Italy. I was stunned. My first impression was that I might not be suitable for that office, and I think that my bishop's thoughts were the same. But I must and I want to put my head before all: and I care more to have a nice place in heaven than a career on earth with prominent positions.[40]

Roncalli arrived in Rome on January 18, 1921, and stayed for four years. His reputation as secretary of Bishop Radini and his pastoral work in Bergamo gave him some prestige in the Rome of Benedict XV (an admirer of Radini) more than in the Rome of Pius X. But leaving Bergamo was "a very big trauma for Roncalli"[41] after fifteen intense and fruitful years in the diocese that included the legacy of Radini Tedeschi, his pastoral work, and his historical studies. The period 1921–1925 was also crucial for Italian history; the Fascist party took power with the conflicted but clear blessing of the Vatican at the expense of the Catholic

---

39. *Diaries 1905–1925*, 458 (November 3, 1919).
40. Ibid., 484 (December 10, 1920).
41. Alberigo, *Papa Giovanni*, 54.

"Partito Popolare," and Italy was under the dictatorship of Benito Mussolini until the end of World War II.

Roncalli's arrival in Rome in 1921 was not easy, and he did not feel at home. The first solemn festivity after his arrival, Easter 1921, was particularly painful. "Easter, full of longing, depression, shock, cold. Hopefully it is the coldness that encloses the life of a better spring."[42] In May 1921 he was appointed domestic prelate of the pope, but wrote that this was an "exterior dignity that gives me a responsibility I feel as a burden."[43]

Roncalli was part of a renewed missionary strategy of Benedict XV that attempted to liberate Catholic missions from the influences of European nations and their growing nationalisms. Following the apostolic letter *Maximum Illud* (November 30, 1919), Rome had become more central in the missionary activity of the local churches. This centralization continued with Pius XI with the motu proprio *Romanorum Pontificum* (May 3, 1922), which Roncalli appears to have some role in drafting. Roncalli was in Rome during this "Romanization" of the missions, in which the role of France in the missionary activity of the church would be diminished. This experience would come to be useful to him in Bulgaria and Turkey.[44]

Roncalli needed to raise money for the missions, which meant an intense travel schedule in all of Italy and beyond. He was sometimes shocked by the material poverty of the churches and dioceses in southern Italy, so distant from the

---

42. *Diaries 1905–1925*, 524 (March 27, 1921).

43. Ibid., 530 (May 11, 1921).

44. See Stefano Trinchese, *Roncalli e le missioni. L'opera della propagazione della fede tra Francia e Vaticano negli anni '20* (Brescia, Italy: Morcelliana, 1989).

Tridentine care of the tidy churches of Lombardia. His travels to France and Germany in December 1921 contributed to the formation of Roncalli as a pastor of a global church and as a church leader with a broad vision of the church's mission in the world. Roncalli learned how to delegate work to others: "To be better able to develop all my work and plans I will remember forever and will practice the Rule of St. Gregory to make others work and not to reserve everything or almost everything to me."[45]

During this time Italy was coming under the dictatorship of Mussolini and of the National Fascist Party. Roncalli wrote to his family, "I cannot find it in my conscience as a Christian and priest to vote for the Fascists. . . .You must do as you wish. My advice is to vote for the Popular [party] list, if there is a free vote. If there is a risk of reprisals, then stay home and leave things alone. Of one thing you can be sure, that the salvation of Italy cannot come about even through Mussolini, clever man as he is. His aims may be good and honest, but the means he employs are wicked and contrary to the laws of the Gospel."[46]

His responsibilities in the church grew; so did the list of his opponents in the Roman Curia, among the French clergy, and in the missionary institutions that had been deprived of their autonomy from the new Roman initiative under Benedict XV. On February 8, 1924, Roncalli received a critical report from his superior, Cardinal Van Rossum. Roncalli commented, "Everything leads me to think that His Eminency is under the assault of someone who is misleading him."[47]

45. Roncalli, *Il Giornale dell'Anima*, 292 (January 1924).
46. *Pope John XXIII, Letters to His Family*, 70 (April 4, 1924).
47. *Diaries 1905–1925*, 553 (February 8, 1924).

His four years of fundraising for missions before the Jubilee of 1925 and the World Missionary Exhibition contributed to Roncalli's visibility but gained him some enemies. Roncalli experienced firsthand not only the importance to do work for the pope in Rome, but also the bureaucratic mentality of the Roman Curia and the plague of ecclesiastical careerism. The lack of coordination within the Roman Curia was evident through his appointment as professor of patristics at the Lateran University shortly before his appointment as a papal diplomat.

This complicated situation for Roncalli in Rome was probably part of his *promoveatur ut amoveatur* to Bulgaria in 1925. His adversaries and opponents in the Roman Curia (especially Cardinal Marchetti Selvaggiani, secretary of Propaganda Fide between 1922 and 1939) and in the Italian Church were likely the origin of the promotion of Angelo Roncalli to the position of "apostolic visitator" in Bulgaria in 1925. Once again, the news was a shock to him, partly because the plan seemed vague with a visit to Bulgaria and then possibly Argentina:

> Cardinal Gasparri, Secretary of State, called me to the Vatican tonight to tell me that it is the will of the Holy Father that I go first to Bulgaria, with episcopal dignity, for a visit to those religious congregations, and then later to South America as apostolic delegate, apparently to Argentina. I asked if this was due obedience. His Eminence told me yes. He added that the proposal was coming from the prefect of the Congregation for the Oriental Churches (Cardinal Tacci). . . . I humbly said that the Holy See found in me an unworthy and unable representative, as I was convinced many others could be sent and likely have more success. I mentioned my sisters, that leaving them would be painful for me. . . . In all it is a great honor for

me unworthy and miserable as I am and this brings no satisfaction to my self-love, but rather spiritual despondency, only tempered by the thought that I did not want nor desire anything of this.[48]

Roncalli was about to begin a very long period (almost thirty years) in which he would be far from Italy—and far from Rome, in particular. Those thirty years left an indelible mark on him. Contacts with other cultures and languages made him a unique and unmatched pope, one who knew a world outside of the geographical boundaries of his own country.

48. Ibid., 567–68 (February 17, 1925).

CHAPTER THREE

Learning from the East: Papal Diplomat in Bulgaria and Turkey

(1925–1944)

After four years in Rome at Propaganda Fide, Angelo Giuseppe Roncalli spent almost the next twenty years of his life (between the ages of forty-four and sixty-three) in eastern Europe, serving more than nine years in Bulgaria and then another nine in Turkey. These countries were geographically and culturally distant and different from Italy; there also were differences between them. This experience shaped Roncalli's understanding of the world outside Catholic Italy, one with different Christian traditions, other religious identities, and a rapidly changing world (socially, culturally, and politically) in the age of dictatorships in Europe leading up to World War II. A few days before his death in May 1963, John XXIII described his experience in eastern Europe as a fundamental part of his walk of life: "It is not that the Gospel has changed; it is that we have begun to understand it better. Those who had similar experiences to my twenty years in eastern Europe and eight in France, and were able to compare different cultures and traditions, know that the moment has come to discern the signs of the times, to seize the opportunity, and to look far ahead."[1]

Roncalli had a clear perception of the role his experience in Bulgaria and Turkey played in his life. On March 12, 1937, after twelve years in Bulgaria, the fifty-five-year-old Roncalli remembered, on the occasion of the liturgical memory of St. Gregory the Great, the pope "whose knowledge of the East yielded an awareness of the world that was of great benefit for him later when he governed the things of the world."[2] That also can be said of Roncalli/John XXIII.

The Unlikely Catholic *Reconquista* of Eastern Europe (Bulgaria, 1925–1934)

Vatican diplomacy makes the Catholic Church different from other Christian churches and other religions. Some of the diplomats of the oldest diplomatic service in the world later became popes, especially in the twentieth century: Achille Ratti, Pius XI; Eugenio Pacelli, Pius XII; and Angelo Giuseppe Roncalli, John XXIII. Roncalli was different from the others because he was sent to very difficult and remote diplomatic posts (Bulgaria and Turkey) without being a professional diplomat; he had not been trained in the special school for Vatican diplomats in Rome, the Pontificia Accademia Ecclesiastica.[3] Roncalli was a well-read priest and

1. Angelo Giuseppe Roncalli, *Il Giornale dell'Anima*, 500 (May 24, 1963).

2. *Diaries Turkey–Greece 1935–1939*, 311 (March 12, 1937).

3. Andrea Riccardi, "Angelo Giuseppe Roncalli, un diplomatico vaticano," *Un cristiano sul trono di Pietro. Studi storici su Papa*

a church historian with a deep admiration for his bishop, Radini Tedeschi of Bergamo; he practiced pastoral ministry in a very traditional, Tridentine way. The diplomatic missions of Roncalli could be easily misjudged as a detour from the life of a pastor and theologian, but they fully belong to the lifelong learning experiences of the last pope who had been a Vatican diplomat.

On February 17, 1925, Cardinal Gasparri, Pius XI's Secretary of State, gave Fr. Roncalli the news of his forthcoming appointment to the post of apostolic visitor in Bulgaria, indicating he would receive the necessary episcopal consecration in order to avoid the difficulties that Achille Ratti (later Pius XI) had gone through with the local episcopate as nuncio in Poland (1918–1921). In a letter to his father on March 3, 1925, Roncalli wrote, "The news is now official: Titular Archbishop of Areopolis and Apostolic Visitor in Bulgaria. Nothing about South America as yet, and I am glad. It only takes a little more than two days by express train, without changing, to get to Bulgaria from Milan. So it is not very far away."[4] Roncalli was consecrated bishop in the church of San Carlo al Corso in Rome on March 19, 1925, by Cardinal Giovanni Tacci, secretary of the Congregation for Oriental Churches. He took his episcopal motto from the church historian Cesare Baronio—*oboedientia et pax* (obedience and peace): "these words represent a little my story and my life."[5]

Giovanni XXIII, Fondazione per le scienze religiose di Bologna, ed. (Gorle: Servitium, 2003), 177–251. See also Francesca Della Salda, *Obbedienza e pace. Il vescovo A. G. Roncallitra Sofia e Roma. (1925–1934)* (Genoa: Marietti, 1989).

4. *Pope John XXIII, Letters to His Family*, trans. Dorothy White (New York/Toronto: McGraw-Hill, 1970), 81 (emphasis mine).

5. Roncalli, *Il Giornale dell'Anima*, 299 (March 13–17, 1925).

Roncalli had no experience with eastern European and Slavic cultures. Neither his education nor his curriculum had prepared him for that part of the world, and he knew that "the church wants to ordain me a bishop in order to send me to Bulgaria as apostolic visitor to exercise a ministry of peace. Maybe I will face many tribulations on my way."[6] But as a church historian, Roncalli was a quick study of eastern Europe and of the complexity of that part of the world. He was not ignorant of eastern Christianity, having spent much time in Rome with the elderly Msgr. Vincenzo Bugarini, expert on the Congregation for the Oriental Churches.[7] But Roncalli was a novice in Vatican diplomacy. Although told he would stay in Bulgaria about six months, he stayed almost ten years.

Roncalli arrived in Sofia, capital of Bulgaria, on April 25, 1925. More experienced Catholic missionaries, such as the French priests Cyrille Korolevskij (François Charon) and the Jesuit Michel d'Herbigny, had been sent from the Vatican to eastern Europe and Russia a few years before. Their intentions and aspirations were less pastoral and ecumenical, and were more focused on gathering intelligence for the dream of a "Catholic *reconquista*" of Eastern Europe.[8] Roncalli quickly realized that the dream of gaining back eastern Europe to Catholicism was impossible, and that his work would be devoted to the restoration of ecumenical unity without forcing the "return to Rome" of non-Catholic

6. Ibid., 297–98 (March 13–17, 1925).

7. Alberto Melloni, *Papa Giovanni. Un cristiano e il suo concilio* (Turin: Einaudi, 2009), 152.

8. See Cyrille Korolevskij, *Kniga bytija moego (Le livre de ma vie). Mémoires autobiographiques, texte établi, édité et annoté par Giuseppe Maria Croce*. Avant-propos du cardinal Jean-Louis Tauran, préface de Étienne Fouilloux (Vatican City: Libreria Editrice Vaticana, 2007) 1:xxix.

Christians. He did that as a pastor and as a diplomat, not as a "specialist" of ecumenism—a pioneering and dangerous branch of Catholic theology before the Second Vatican Council.[9]

Roncalli's challenges went beyond leaving Rome and his home country of Italy for a distant, poor, and non-Catholic country; they had more to do with the lack of clarity in the diplomatic instructions for the apostolic delegate. These challenges included the connections between Vatican diplomacy and the national interests of Italy and France in the Balkans, in the midst of fierce nationalistic sentiments in countries like Bulgaria that were humiliated by the end of the Ottoman Empire and the result of World War I; the growing difference of views between the Roman dream of "taking back" eastern Europe from the Orthodox Church; and the distance between Roncalli's deep appreciation of the traditions of eastern Christianity and the official stance of Rome toward non-Catholic and non-Roman Catholic churches. Although the Orthodox churches were weakened by the Soviet revolution in Russia, Roncalli did not believe in a Catholic *reconquista* of eastern Europe.[10]

It was not clear whether Roncalli's appointment to the diplomatic post in Bulgaria resulted from difficulties in his work at the Curia Congregation of Propaganda Fide in Rome. But it was clear that Bulgaria was a peripheric and

9. In September 1925 Roncalli encouraged the Congregation for the Oriental Churches to read the speech given by the Bulgarian metropolitan Stephan at the ecumenical conference in Stockholm ("Congrès de l'Alliance Universelle pour le Rapprochement des Églises") for what Stephan said about the Catholic Church. See ASV, Affari Ecclesiastici Straordinari, periodo IV: Bulgaria, P.O. 10.

10. Étienne Fouilloux, *Les catholiques et l'unité chrétienne du XIXe au XXe siècle: itinéraires européens d'expression francaise* (Paris: Le Centurion, 1982), 75.

secondary destination, even if Bulgaria had been geopolitically crucial in the pre-World War II Balkans. Since the beginning of the fourteenth century, Bulgaria had been part of the Ottoman Empire. Bulgaria gained independence in 1878, but the ambitions of the country to become the "Great Bulgaria" had been frustrated by German chancellor Bismarck at the Berlin Conference of June–July 1878.[11] In 1912–1913 Bulgaria had been involved in the first Balkan War only to see its borders once again redrawn at the end of the war, making its religious geography even more complicated. In 1923 a coup d'etat (there was another one in 1934) banned democratic parties, and when Msgr. Roncalli arrived in Sofia, the country was in a politically tense situation. Ten days before his arrival in Sofia, the capital was the target of a terrorist attack that blew up the Cathedral of Sofia and claimed 128 lives.[12]

Roncalli's mission to Bulgaria was also precarious because of the disrepair of the facilities and structures available to the apostolic visitor. In a letter to Cardinal Luigi Sincero (his direct superior, the secretary for the Roman Congregation for the Oriental Churches) a few weeks after his arrival, Roncalli described the residence of the papal diplomat as a house subject to frequent flooding and inhabitated by small animals. It was a residence that he had to share with Constantine Bosschaerts, a Benedictine from the Netherlands, and two Bulgarian priests, Josaphat Kozarov and Stephen Kurtev.

11. Vincenzo Criscuolo, *Roberto Menini (1837–1916). Arcivescovo cappuccino Vicario Apostolico di Sofia e Plovdiv* (Trento: Biblioteca Provinciale dei Cappuccini, 2006), 155–62.

12. Angelo Giuseppe Roncalli, *Lettere ai familiari 1901–1962*, ed. Loris Francesco Capovilla (Rome: Edizioni di Storia e Letteratura, 1968) vol. 1, 117.

Besides these logistical issues, Roncalli's major problem in Bulgaria was the silence from Rome, even when the inexperienced apostolic visitor asked for help or feedback on his initiatives. Being ignored and left alone by Rome caused sorrow in Roncalli: "I was ordained a bishop twenty months ago. As it was easy to foresee, my ministry has given me many tribulations. But ironically they do not come from the Bulgarians for whom I work, but from the central organs of ecclesiastical administration [the Roman Curia]. It is a form of mortification and humiliation that I did not expect, and that hurts me very very much. O Lord, You know everything [*Domine, tu omnia nosti*]."[13]

Roncalli received a list of priorities from the Vatican at the time of his appointment: the visit to the Catholic communities of refugees from Tracia and Macedonia in Bulgaria; the selection of a bishop for Bulgarian Catholics of Eastern Rite; the foundation of a seminary for the formation of local clergy; and the pastoral care of religious orders in Bulgaria.[14] But Roncalli found it difficult to get Rome to react to any news and updates about his work in Bulgaria. This aspect of his work had an impact on Roncalli's view of the government of the church, which turned out to be useful when he was elected pope in 1958.

The uncertainty of the vision of the diplomatic mission entrusted to Roncalli by the Holy See allowed him—or maybe

13. Roncalli, *Il Giornale dell'Anima*, 302 (November–December 1926).

14. See Angelo Giuseppe Roncalli, *Il lupo, l'orso, l'agnello: epistolario bulgaro con don K. Raev e mons. D. Theelen*, ed. Paolo Cortesi (Cinisello Balsamo, Milan: San Paolo, 2013); see also Kiril Plamen Kartaloff, *La sollecitudine ecclesiale di monsignor Roncalli in Bulgaria (1925–1934)* (Città del Vaticano: Libreria Editrice Vaticana, 2014).

moved him—toward a broad interpretation of his mandate. Not limited to the tasks of diplomatic relations with the government, King Boris III, and the other diplomatic missions in Bulgaria, Roncalli traveled across the country. It was his opportunity to assess a current reality that was historically, politically, socially, and religiously complex, an interwoven history of conflicts between nations and religions in an area wedged between difficult borders: Europe (Greece to the south and the area west of the Austro-Hungarian Empire), the north (Romania and most of Ukraine under the Soviet Union, historically Orthodox territory), and the southeast (the Turkish power struggling with a policy of forced westernization necessitated by the defeat in World War I and the end of the Ottoman Empire). Thanks to the long-distance passenger train the Orient Express, which traveled from Milan/Venice to Sofia/Belgrade, Roncalli went regularly to Italy to his Sotto il Monte for the holidays and to Rome more than once a year, on missions to Constantinople, and on retreats to preach to religious communities.

Roncalli's experience in Bulgaria was one of "otherness."[15] But this otherness had very concrete issues. The first problem of Bulgarian Catholicism was the national question. The central issue was the link between nation and religious confession: Bulgaria had an Orthodox majority, but also various Catholic communities. Bulgarian Catholicism only numbered about 35,000 faithful, including a majority of Catholics belonging to the Latin Rite supported by religious congregations related to the leaders of the western powers (especially France), and a "Uniate" Catholic minority, unwanted both by Latin Catholics and by the Orthodox Church of Bulgaria.

15. Valeria Martano, "L'Oriente come esperienza della alterità nella vita di Roncalli," *Un cristiano sul trono di Pietro*, 73–115.

Roncalli's rejection of religious nationalism was motivated not only by the experience of its tragic fruits in World War I, but also by an ecclesiology strongly loyal to Rome on the basis of a historical/political vision driven by the dream of a union of Christian nations around the pope. As explained by the French priest Cyrille Korolevskij, who later became Eastern Catholic, Roncalli experienced the impossibility to serve the church and a nationalistic cause at the same time. By the time Roncalli was in Bulgaria, his writings had already begun to reject the conflation of nation, religion, Catholicism, and ideology. His Bulgarian experience—contact with refugees and age-old sectarian hatreds—further shaped Roncalli's dismissal of religious nationalism and an acceptance of a global world, a global Christianity, and a global Catholicism, *ante litteram*.[16] These ideas became part of the worldview of the future John XXIII, far from the fascinations of "political religion" typical of the Fascist-era clerical culture in Europe. Roncalli's experiences of World War I, the ethnic-national upheavals of postwar totalitarianism, and World War II did not turn into a populistic contempt of politics. As a diplomat, Roncalli was very aware of the tangible coexistence and the historical space between earthly powers and the churches, even in eastern Europe, which had been only tangentially touched by the post-Tridentine process of "confessionalization" between the sixteenth and twentieth centuries. Roncalli avoided placing the church in a parallel and completely separate world.

16. Alfredo Canavero, "Le aperture al mondo: Giovanni XXIII e le grandi potenze in conflitto," *L'ora che sta il mondo attraversando. Giovanni XXIII di fronte alla storia*, eds. Giovanni Grado Merlo and Francesco Mores (Rome: Edizioni di Storia e Letteratura, 2009), 227–46.

In the Europe of nationalism between the two world wars, Roncalli saw the influence and damage done by national interests conveyed and defended by Catholic institutions with national allegiances. The French presence was crucial in Bulgaria in the 1920s as it was at the same time in "modern China," founded after the break of 1919, in which the apostolic delegate Celso Costantini had to struggle against the privileges of French missionaries in front of China-born Catholic clergy and against French meddling in Chinese politics. If it were true that the system of national protectorates for Catholic missionaries expired in 1914 in the East, and that the Peace of Lausanne had abolished the "capitulations" (protections granted by Western colonial powers to Christian missions), the situation in Bulgaria was far from having dissolved all ties with the recent past. Moreover, French Catholics in Bulgaria constituted a further line of fracture within the already jagged ecclesiastical situation of Catholics in that country. This situation tempted many Bulgarians to involve the Catholic Church in partisan politics, something Roncalli firmly refused:

> It was my duty to warn the clergy against any involvement in electoral matters, and for my part I thought it best *détourner* from my residence a small movement that was mentioned for an organization of Bulgarian Catholics for the appointment of a deputy of ours [*a Catholic parliamentarian*]. The subjects I know well are not reliable in these matters. We should still work long before the political consciousness of these Catholics is ready for similar experiments. Every political pronouncement could be extremely negative to Catholic interests in a situation like this where fundamental principles relating to the life of the church are not at stake. It would also be extremely dangerous if anyone

could suspect or give the impression that the papal representative is more or less involved in electoral matters.[17]

Linked to the problem of the presence of foreigners and religious orders related to the western powers was the dynastic question, which for Roncalli was the most difficult test of his Bulgarian period. The election of a Catholic, Ferdinand of Saxony-Coburg-Gotha-Kohary, as Prince of Bulgaria on July 7, 1887, and Tsar in 1908, by the Bulgarian National Assembly had opened high hopes in Rome for the "return" of Orthodox Bulgaria to Catholicism. But the decision to convert Ferdinand's two-year-old firstborn, Boris III, to Orthodoxy in 1896 interrupted this dream and brought the Bulgarian royal family recognition by the European powers.

After the rude awakening from the dream of a re-Catholicization of Bulgaria through dynastic relations of the Holy See with the Bulgarian government, the Vatican in the 1920s attempted to influence, through amendments to the legislation on cults, the state of relations between Catholicism and Orthodoxy. Roncalli had frequent meetings with members of the government about education laws and religious freedom for Bulgarian Catholics, a question that had already been raised in 1910–1911 by Italian diplomats in Bulgaria, when a bill of the Bulgarian government was judged unfair to Catholics by the Holy See (and was later withdrawn). In the same period initial attempts were made to compile a dossier for a concordat between Bulgaria and the Holy See, but in 1911 it was considered impracticable, given the fact that the royal family had moved back to Orthodoxy.

17. Report of Roncalli to Cardinal Pacelli, June 9, 1931, in ASV, Delegazione Apostolica Bulgaria, 4, G, 1931.

Roncalli wrote in 1925 about the outlook for a concordat with Bulgaria; realistically he considered it very unlikely.

At the beginning of his mission Roncalli did not object to the project of a renewed union of Christianity under Rome, but the pastoral dimension of his apostolic visit represented the counterpart of his life in Bulgaria. Roncalli desired to do pastoral work besides the delicate political and diplomatic issues that had to be addressed. Early in his time in Bulgaria, Roncalli was struck by the miserable state of ecclesiastical discipline in Bulgaria, especially with respect to obedience and chastity among the clergy, and the poverty of the country in general, which pushed him to strive for emergency relief (for events such as the devastating earthquake of April 14, 1928). In a situation complicated by the overlap of different ecclesiastical jurisdictions (divided on the basis of different liturgical rites, territories, and national affiliation), many parts of Bulgaria had forgotten basic elements of ecclesiastical discipline—and they also felt forgotten by Rome.[18] Roncalli saw situations that had been common in the messy Catholic Church in western Europe before the enactment of the reforms of the Council of Trent.

The consequences from the wars of the previous decade, the moving boundaries, and the resulting displacement of populations influenced the apostolic visitor to group Bulgarian Catholic refugees "together to not get lost among the schismatics." But the official terminology of the time defining non-Catholics as "schismatics" did not prevent the

18. See the report prepared by Roncalli and sent to the Roman Congregation of Propaganda Fide, dated February 24, 1926: ASV, Archivio della Delegazione Apostolica in Bulgaria, busta 2 (24 febbraio 1926). *Relazione della visita apostolica alle missioni latine della Bulgaria inviata a Propaganda Fide.*

visitor Roncalli to forge relationships with the local Orthodox hierarchy, which was stunned by the amazing addresses
of the apostolic visitor to the meetings of the Holy Synod
of the Bulgarian Orthodox Church. A few weeks after his
arrival in Bulgaria, on August 26, 1925, Roncalli had sent
a message to the Synod of the Orthodox Church of Bulgaria—an unprecedented kind of message coming from a
Vatican diplomat to a "schismatic" church.

The major success of Roncalli's mission in Bulgaria was the
appointment of Stephen Kurtev to apostolic administrator for
the Bulgarian Catholics of the Eastern Rite (Uniate) in 1926,
which helped to overcome the crisis within the Catholic
Church in Bulgaria after the end of World War I. But during
Roncalli's entire tenure in Sofia, his work was made difficult
by the lack of clarity from the Vatican on the priorities of his
mission, and especially for the allocation of funds. Already in
the summer of 1925 Roncalli showed irritation when he wrote
this letter to Msgr. Borgongini Duca of the Roman Curia
Congregation for Extraordinary Ecclesiastical Affairs:

> Dear Monsignor, you remember how I was sent here in
> haste because it was urgent to provide someone immedi-
> ately to the diplomatic post, to investigate things on the
> spot and to present projects. I submitted my clear and
> detailed plans more than three months ago. . . . I know
> that in Rome it takes time to make decisions. But at least
> write a few words to give me some ideas about the general
> horizons of my mission . . . or at least invite me to be
> patient . . . or give me a tip on some event or personal
> matter for which I've begged and pleaded. . . . But noth-
> ing. . . . Tell me, Monsignor, what should I do? . . . It has
> been more than twelve months that poor me is doing hard
> work. The four months spent in visits around Bulgaria were
> a source of great spiritual comfort, but I was also physically

tired. . . . Because I want to do things as a good son, despite the silence and the near abandonment of my Congregation for Oriental Churches, I beg you, Monsignor, to help me, at the level of the Holy Father directly or with somebody who may authorize if, as I believe, we need authorization, because it may be granted also to the poor Apostolic Visitor to Bulgaria what [the Roman Curia] gives even to the hardly fatigued canon priests of Rome.[19]

The misunderstandings continued until 1929, especially with Cardinal Sincero of the Congregation for Oriental Churches regarding the use of funds for the works of the pontifical mission. The frustration of Roncalli also emerged from his notes taken during spiritual retreats:

The spiritual pains in the past months through which the Lord wanted to try my patience for practices about the founding of the Bulgarian seminary; my uncertainty that has lasted for more than five years regarding the duties of my ministry in this country; concerns and the difficulty of not being able to do more and having to live a life of a perfect hermit against the tendency of my spirit to do work in the direct ministry of souls; inner discontent of what is still human in my nature, even though so far I managed to keep it in discipline; all this makes more spontaneous my holy abandonment, which would like to be a spiritual rise and impulse toward a more perfect imitation of my Divine Exemplar.[20]

19. Letter of Roncalli to Msgr. Borgongini Duca, secretary of the Congregation for Ecclesiastical Extraordinary Affairs, August 26, 1925, in ASV, Archivio della Delegazione Apostolica Bulgaria, busta 5.
20. Roncalli, *Il Giornale dell'Anima*, 313–14 (April–May 1930).

Another serious misunderstanding with the Roman Curia, which turned out to be the major diplomatic failure of Roncalli's mission to Bulgaria, concerned the intention of the Vatican to take back to Catholicism the kingdom of Bulgaria via the marriage of King Boris with an Italian Catholic princess, Giovanna of Savoy. The marriage took place in Assisi on October 25, 1930, but once back in Bulgaria, King Boris had his marriage celebrated for a second time according to the rite of the Orthodox Church, which was a statement about his intention not to convert to Catholicism, thus contradicting his previous promises.

Despite this diplomatic setback for the Holy See, Roncalli's position was elevated. On September 26, 1931, the mission to Bulgaria was promoted from "apostolic visitor" to "apostolic delegate"—the first apostolic delegate in the history of the relationship between the Holy See and Bulgaria. But his difficulty with Rome continued and, as a consequence, Roncalli found it difficult to help the Bulgarian people and refugees in an international situation that was getting worse. The conditions of backwardness in Bulgaria and the situation of Bulgarian Catholicism—the will to make that church independent from the French protection and the concomitant global economic crisis of the early 1930s—pushed Roncalli to turn to Rome for funds, given that the flow of aid from the United States (coming mostly from Francis Spellman, future cardinal archbishop of New York), the royal house, and the religious orders related to the powers of western Europe had greatly decreased compared to the decades prior.[21]

---

21. See the dramatic letter of Michel d'Herbigny from the Vatican Commission *Pro Russia* to Roncalli of January 21, 1932, in ASV, Delegazione Apostolica Bulgaria, 21.

The international economic crisis also had an impact on the ability of Roncalli to keep in touch with his family. The relationship between Roncalli and his family was not interrupted, but the manner and frequency of the visits changed. Holiday periods spent in Sotto il Monte and the regular shipment of money to help his sisters (whose amount changed during the global economic crisis after 1929) attest to the assiduity of a personal relationship with the clergy of Bergamo and with his family. Several times his sisters spent long periods in Sofia living with him in the residence.

Traveling to Italy allowed Roncalli to maintain contact with his family and the diocese, and also with the Roman Curia, with which Roncalli had many misunderstandings. In the young diplomat's notes, Roncalli's enthusiasm was evident for his mission and his will to undertake concrete projects for the Bulgarian church (a new home for the diplomatic residence, the land, and a project for the new seminary). But Roncalli was afflicted by the economic uncertainty and, more generally, the uncertainty about the duration and purpose of his mission in Bulgaria and the possibility of making long-term plans. Between the end of 1932 and the beginning of 1933, rumors in the Curia caused Roncalli to think about a promotion to the diocese of Brescia (in northern Italy, not far from his birthplace) or a transfer to the diplomatic post in Bucharest, Romania.[22] Roncalli sometimes took these rumors as an implicit criticism of his tenure in Bulgaria, sometimes as another signal of uncertainty about his future.

22. Maria Carosio, "L'apprendistato diplomatico di Istanbul (1931–1935)," *Angelo Dell'Acqua, prete, diplomatico e cardinale al cuore della politica vaticana (1903–1972)*, ed. Alberto Melloni (Bologna: il Mulino, 2004), 65–75.

Roncalli's tenure in Bulgaria was more difficult with the challenges coming from the Roman Curia than from the huge problems of Bulgarian Catholicism and of Bulgaria as a country. But the mission to Bulgaria made Roncalli an experienced Vatican diplomat. In August 1934 it seemed that Roncalli did not know that the rumors about his transfer this time were true. In his retreat of August 1934 in Russe (or Routschouk) with the Passionist Fathers, Roncalli wrote these words about the prospects of his ministry in Bulgaria:

> The circumstances of my ministry as it unfolded after ten years of living in Bulgaria do not recommend me, nor allow me to do something different from what I do, at least for now. So I will continue to live day by day, but providing you with the most ardent passion, Jesus, this my life so that I must impose this restriction to my outward activity, and all my life of intense prayer, to the salvation and to the sanctification of my soul and of these bishops and priests, for deeper spread and penetration of the spirit of charity in this country, where there is so much bitterness in all, for the edification and religious progress of the Catholic faithful, in light of all this blessing and Bulgarian people, misled, and yet so full of good attitudes toward the kingdom of Christ and of his church. What did Monsignor Roncalli do in the monotony of his life during his tenure at the apostolic delegation? In the sanctification of himself, in simplicity, goodness, and joy, he has opened a source of blessings and graces—that will continue even after his death—for the whole of Bulgaria.[23]

23. Roncalli, *Il Giornale dell'Anima,* 330 (August 1934).

"My Eyes Witness a Social Palingenesis": Turkey and Greece (1935–1944)

Roncalli was shocked with the news on November 17, 1934, of his appointment as apostolic delegate to Turkey and Greece. His official residence would be in Istanbul, formerly Constantinople, which for more than ten centuries (until 1453) had been the capital of the eastern Roman Empire and of eastern Christianity. Based on the neglect by the Roman Curia for almost ten years in Bulgaria, Roncalli's move to the capital of the newly ultra-secularist and nationalist Turkey could not be interpreted as a promotion. Roncalli saw his new diplomatic post as the appointment to celebrate "the funeral of a splendid past, now completely gone"—the splendid past of eastern Christianity.[24]

Roncalli had traveled between Sofia and Turkey many times, but when he arrived in Istanbul on January 5, 1935, he was there to stay. The life of the papal diplomat in Istanbul was not easy: "I have left that land [Bulgaria] with my heart full of joy that I served there and dedicated ten years of my life to those precious souls. In Constantinople, as you know, times are hard. I did not want anyone to come to the station. . . . Do not fear for me. Here I am much happier that I was in Sofia, because I have more scope for my work as priest and bishop."[25]

Roncalli wrote in his diary about his first full day in Istanbul: "The day was consoling as a whole. Some thorns are visible here and there, but *in charitate et lenitate*, with God's help, we hope to make good progress."[26] Roncalli was

24. *Diaries Turkey–Greece 1935–1939*, xi.
25. Letter to his parents from Constantinople, January 8, 1935, *Pope John XXIII, Letters to His Family*, 245.
26. *Diaries Turkey–Greece 1935–1939*, 10 (January 6, 1935).

probably hinting at the difficult legacy his predecessor in the diplomatic post, Msgr. Margotti, had left him, especially concerning the relationship with the Turkish government. Compared to the religious landscape he had known in the overwhelmingly Orthodox Bulgaria, Turkey was more complicated. There were only 30,000 Catholics in the country, and they were divided by the practice of different liturgical rites (Latin, Armenian, Chaldean, Greek, Syriac, and Melkite). They were mostly French-speaking and non-Turkish by ethnical origins, which made them look even more foreign in the eyes of the young and vibrant Turkish nationalism. Moreover, the Catholic community in Turkey was divided among different national interests in the area (especially Italy and France) that made the Catholic presence suspect. It was perceived as a foreign intelligence agency with the difference that these foreigners (Catholic priests and Vatican diplomats included) could not speak Turkish and were even more divided among a myriad of small religious orders vying for supremacy in the small Catholic flock. Istanbul was the see of both the Orthodox Patriarch of Constantinople and the Armenian patriarchate, one of the largest Jewish communities in the Mediterranean area, and a legacy of the Ottoman Empire. Istanbul was also a safe haven for refugees from Stalin's purges and from the Nazi regime. In 1935, Istanbul was not an intellectual backwater, but a cosmopolitan city with a thriving community of scholars and libraries, where humanism survived while it was being expelled from Europe.[27]

27. The decade of Roncalli in Istanbul almost completely overlaps with the decade spent there by the German philologist Eric Auerbach (1892–1957), the author of the seminal work *Mimesis* (1946). Recent studies on Auerbach suggest that the two met and that Auerbach

The new regime of Mustafa Kemal "Atatürk" (literally "father of the Turks") that took over Turkey after the collapse of the Ottoman Empire at the end of World War I was marked by a visible and ideological secularist agenda effectively and rapidly banning every religious presence from the public square in the attempt to modernize the country via an eradication of the public role of Islam. As an apostolic delegate he could not accomplish the mission to sign a concordat between the Apostolic See and Turkey and Greece. A concordat was the centerpiece of Vatican diplomacy during the twentieth century, especially under Pius XI and Pius XII. Roncalli's mission to Turkey and Greece was a diplomatic one and also a pastoral one. Roncalli's task was complicated even more by the fact that his portfolio as a papal diplomat extended to the small Catholic community in Greece where the situation for the Catholic Church was even more difficult due to the confessionalist regime in favor of the Greek Orthodox Church and the anti-Catholic policies that had been put in place. The "exchange of populations" of 1923 between Turkey and Greece was one of the first experiences of ethnic cleansing, and the Armenian population in Turkey and in the area suffered the first genocide in modern history.

This extremely complicated situation reinforced Roncalli's view to separate Catholicism from nationalism and to distance Vatican diplomacy and politics from particular national interests. That did not mean Roncalli's attitude meant detachment from the political, social, and cultural aspects of his mission. On the contrary, he developed a deep love for the people he met: "I love the Turkish people, and

---

helped Roncalli in his efforts to save Balkan Jews. See Arthur Krystal, "The Book of Books," *The New Yorker* (December 9, 2013): 83–88.

I appreciate the natural qualities of this people that prepared a place in the path of civilization."[28] In Turkey, Roncalli saw the quick pace of change in politics, society, and culture: "My eyes witness a social palingenesis among the most remarkable in the history of peoples."[29]

Compared to his years in Bulgaria, in Turkey and Greece Roncalli had fewer occasions to meet with government public officials, but had more contacts with the "religious other," especially Orthodox Christians and Jews.[30] As a Vatican diplomat and a Catholic bishop, Roncalli understood earlier and more thoroughly than others the objectives of modern Catholicism in a globalized world: the need to make eastern Catholics a real "local church"; less dependence on the political and institutional support of the western diplomacy in the area; the dangers of the conflation of religion and nationalism in light of recent, violent historical experience; the opportunities provided by ecumenical dialogue and by interreligious relations to grow in the understanding of the Gospel and of Christianity itself.

This set of objectives gave Roncalli many opportunities to deepen his understanding of the role and mission of the church and its ministries in a growingly interconnected world. Roncalli learned that he had more to fear from the Greek confessionalist regime of an established Orthodox Church than from the secularist agenda of the Turkish regime

28. Roncalli, *Il Giornale dell'Anima*, 344 (November 12–18, 1939).
29. Loris Capovilla, *Giovanni XXIII: Quindici letture* (Rome: 1970) 113.
30. David Bankier, "Roncalli e gli ebrei prima di Israele," and Ilaria Pavan, "Roncalli e gli ebrei dalla Shoah alla Declaratio Nostra Aetate. Tracce di un percorso," *L'ora che sta il mondo attraversando*, 263–73; 275–300.

of Atatürk (even with a law in 1935 forcing all the clergy to give up religious vestments and to wear "modern" clothes). Turkey was a vast laboratory for the coexistence of Catholics as a tiny minority surrounded by other Christian minorities and an almost totally Muslim population governed by French-educated modernizers. Roncalli studied Turkish in order to do both his work as a papal diplomat and as a Catholic bishop with pastoral duties. In his report to Cardinal Pacelli on May 25, 1935, Roncalli lamented, "Despite all the invitations of the Holy See (more insistent in recent times) to recruit local seminarians to become missionaries to Turkey and learn the language of the country, here we are still at the beginning [in the original Italian: *tabula rasa*]. There is not one who speaks Turkish; if someone speaks Turkish, it is by accident and an exception."[31]

Roncalli was able to look at Turkey with an approach different from that of the Tridentine period (especially the sixteenth and seventeenth centuries), when Turkish was the language of the political and religious enemies *par excellence* for Catholics. But Roncalli retained some of the elements of a Catholic culture that saw in Catholicism also a *mission civilisatrice*. Roncalli, as many other Catholics, saw in the colonial wars of Italy in eastern Africa (1935–1936) an opportunity to expand the presence of the Gospel.[32]

A few decades before the emergence of the "theology of the local church" at Vatican II, Roncalli wanted to make the small communities of eastern Catholics real local churches, with a proper diocesan dimension. In Turkey Roncalli was even more convinced of the need to bring some kind of unity between different churches and different religions. In 1936

31. *Diaries Turkey–Greece 1935–1939*, xv.
32. Ibid., 141–42 (March 2, 1936).

he was a pilgrim to Mount Athos in Greece and managed to stay in Greece (a country particularly difficult for a Vatican diplomat to enter) a few weeks, which was longer than he expected.

An advocate of inculturation of Catholics (based on an understanding of the term typical of the 1930s), Roncalli experienced his diplomatic and pastoral ministry as an itinerant ministry, traveling often and covering long distances to encounter his people and to know better the country. Between March and December of 1938 Roncalli was making pastoral visits to the Catholic communities in Turkey. His mission never became one to convert eastern Europe to Catholicism as many in the Vatican wanted, especially after the collapse of the Orthodox Church in imperial Russia after 1917. Roncalli discouraged the conversions of Orthodox Christians to Catholicism, not only because he was afraid of a possible backlash against Catholics accused of proselytism, but he wanted prospective converts to go deeper in the understanding of their own Orthodox tradition, which he did not see as schismatic. It is noteworthy that Roncalli tended to avoid the official label of "schismatics" for Orthodox Christians, even in his official correspondence with the Vatican. He preferred "Orthodox," "Orthodox brothers," or "Greeks." That was not the only point of distinction between Roncalli and the Roman Curia. The misunderstandings that had caused his years in Bulgaria to be so difficult persisted as apostolic delegate to Turkey and Greece. Even in 1936, eleven years after his initial appointment in the East, he wrote, "It pains me to see the distance between my way of looking at situations here and the way Rome looks at these situations; it is my only real cross."[33]

33. Roncalli, *Il Giornale dell'Anima*, 334 (October 13–16, 1936).

The first five years of Roncalli's time in Turkey were focused on the pastoral and ecclesial dimensions of his mission; the second part, between 1939 and 1944, was absorbed by the war. In the middle of this time, the deaths of *his* pope, Pius XI and, a few weeks earlier, his mother Marianna, marked 1939 as a year of change for Roncalli. Roncalli's diplomatic work in Turkey and his frequent contacts with Rome become even more important with the approaching war caused by nationalistic and racist regimes in Europe (Italy and Germany). His schedule became much busier and his presence in Turkey was crucial for Vatican diplomacy. Roncalli's agenda became focused on two major items: the relationship with the Turkish government and, more so, the threatening presence of Nazi Germany occupying eastern Europe and areas in the Mediterranean.

The death of Pius XI and the election of Pius XII on March 2, 1939, gave Roncalli the opportunity to send a message to the Orthodox Patriarchate of Constantinople. It was the first official exchange between the Roman Catholic and the Orthodox Church since they had excommunicated each other in the year 1054. Roncalli's initiative was successful. For the commemoration of Pius XI the presence of guests was notable: the entire diplomatic corps including representatives of the Patriarch of Constantinople, the Armenian-Gregorian bishop, the Grand Rabbi of Istanbul, and the president of the Jewish community of Istanbul.[34] In May 1939 the apostolic delegate met with the Patriarch of Constantinople; this was Roncalli's masterpiece, a historic achievement with huge implications both theologically and diplomatically.

34. Alberto Melloni, *Tra Istanbul, Atene e la guerra*, (Genoa: Marietti, 1993) 186.

Roncalli's network of contacts proved crucial during the war for his effort to save Jewish refugees from eastern Europe. After 1941 Roncalli was able to more easily visit Greece (July–October 1941) and also the Italian soldiers, allies of Nazi Germany, occupying Greece.[35] He did not witness the great deportation of the Jews from Thessaloniki in 1943. Turkey remained neutral during World War II, and it became a natural venue for diplomatic exchanges, covert meetings, and political operations of many kinds, including the rescue of Jews fleeing from Nazi-occupied eastern Europe. Roncalli had very few opportunities to meet with Jews in his home country, but his deep appreciation for the Jewish people grew during the war. This bore fruit through the rescue of thousands of Jews between 1942 and 1944 and also after the war as a bishop and a pope, with a deep appreciation—much deeper than his predecessors on the chair of Peter—of the role of Jews and Judaism for Catholic theology and the Catholic Church. In January 1943 Roncalli received a memo from Rabbi Chayim Barlas about the proportions of the Shoah and the need of the apostolic delegate's help to save Jews. During that year Roncalli met several times with Barlas, the Grand Rabbi of Istanbul, Markus, and representatives of the Jewish Agency for Palestine.[36]

In Turkey before the beginning of the war, Roncalli had spoken against racism in a famous homily that worried the diplomat corp of Italy, which in November 1938 had passed the "racial laws" banning Italian Jews from every aspect of public life in Italy. In the famous (but now lost) homily of January 6, 1939, Roncalli affirmed that the church had

---

35. *Diaries Turkey–Greece 1940–1944*, 362–68 (March 1942).
36. Ibid., 497–659, passim.

ignored the separation of humanity by race and stressed the impossibility for the church to become a racist church.[37]

Roncalli experienced firsthand the moral complexity of the anti-Nazi and antiracist stance of the church. Catholics were fighting in every army in World War II in Europe, except in the Red Army of the Soviet Union, and the Communist threat was perceived as the ultimate danger for the future not only of Catholicism, but also of humanity. The testimony that Roncalli gave of his meeting with Pope Pius XII in the Vatican on October 10, 1941, was shocking: "Rome. Audience with the Holy Father . . . who was very lovable. He spoke with me at length about his magnanimity [in the original Italian: *larghezza di tratto*] with the Germans who come to visit him. He asked me whether his silence about the behavior of the Nazis is not judged negatively [in the original Italian: *giudicato male*]."[38]

Between 1942 and 1944 it became difficult to travel to Italy. Roncalli's world was more limited to Istanbul, where he worked for the humanitarian goal of saving the lives of many refugees from eastern Europe: Jews, but also Polish and Greek political refugees. He had direct contacts with

37. The text of this homily is now lost, but in the following days it sparked many reactions among the Jewish community, the diplomatic corp, and Italian politicians. See *Diaries Turkey–Greece 1935–1939*, 619; Melloni, *Tra Istanbul, Atene e la guerra*, 183.

38. *Diaries Turkey–Greece 1940–1944*, 290; Melloni, *Tra Istanbul, Atene e la guerra*, 240–41. The literature on the relationship between Pius XII and the Nazi regime is vast and often biased in both directions. Frank J. Coppa, *The Life and Pontificate of Pope Pius XII. Between History and Controversy* (Washington DC: The Catholic University of America Press, 2013) and Robert A. Ventresca, *Soldier of Christ. The Life of Pope Pius XII* (Cambridge, MA: Belknap Press of Harvard University Press, 2013).

the Jewish Agency and the Red Crescent, but also with the emissaries of Nazi Germany. Roncalli had to deal with the more than ambiguous Franz von Papen—a Catholic politician, former chancellor of Germany, and member of the Nazi regime who was the German ambassador to Turkey. At the beginning of the war Roncalli thought that the best strategy for the clergy in Turkey was to walk a fine line: "Very little politics, respect for the nationality of all, and a search for God's judgement in everything."[39] This period was important for Roncalli to build his network of contacts with many prelates of the Orthodox hierarchy in Greece and the Orthodox Patriarchate in Istanbul.

Roncalli's years in the East were a significant experience for the Vatican diplomat and significantly deepened his knowledge of the fathers of the church (both Latin and Greek) and the traditions of eastern Christianity. During this time Roncalli continued to work at the edition of the acts of the apostolic visit of St. Charles Borromeo to the diocese of Bergamo.[40] Roncalli also deepened his understanding of Christianity from a historical point of view, which he had started to develop under bishop Radini Tedeschi in Bergamo and by witnessing events of epochal significance such as the secularization of Turkey and World War II. But the time of isolation from Italy and of incomprehension from the

---

39. *Diaries Turkey–Greece 1935–1939*, 730 (September 23, 1939).

40. First volume published in 1936: Angelo Giuseppe Roncalli, *Atti della visita apostolica di S. Carlo Borromeo a Bergamo (1575)* (Florence: Olschki, 1936–1958 [but 1959], 5 volumes). In 1939 Roncalli published a history of the diocesan seminary in Bergamo and on the role of seminaries in the teaching of the Council of Trent: *Gli inizi del seminario di Bergamo e San Carlo Borromeo. Note storiche con una introduzione sul concilio di Trento e la fondazione dei primi seminari* (Bergamo: Società Anonima Editrice S. Alessandro, 1939).

Vatican was for Roncalli a sort of protracted spiritual exercise in search of a Catholicism becoming global. Roncalli merged his historical awareness and knowledge of church history with the simple and traditional devotional and liturgical style of a priest trained according to the guidelines of Tridentine Catholicism. His understanding of the Catholic tradition benefited from his encounter with other cultures and churches and from his direct experience of the disasters originating from religious/ecclesiastical nationalism. Roncalli developed a deep conviction about the connection between peace among nations and the ecumenical unity of churches and religions. In his famous Pentecost homily of 1944 he expressed this vision:

> We like to distinguish ourselves from those who do not profess our faith or practice our traditions and liturgies: Orthodox brethren, Protestants, Jews, Muslims, and believers or nonbelievers of other religions. I understand that diversity of race, language, and education is a painful reminder of a sad past that kept us mutually at a distance. . . . My dear brothers and sons, I must tell you that in the light of the Gospel and the Catholic principle, this logic is false.[41]

Roncalli rejected the nationalist and racist appropriations of the Gospel that were typical of the end of European Christendom in the twentieth century. Instead, it was a spirituality of unity and communion beyond the nations, races, and religions that shaped his life—and, therefore, the church of Vatican II.

41. The whole text of the homily in *Predicazione a Istanbul*, 366–73.

CHAPTER FOUR

Between the "Exile" and the Final Ascent: France and Venice

(1945–1958)

On December 6, 1944, while in Istanbul, Roncalli received a telegram from Rome announcing his appointment as apostolic nuncio in Paris: "I am surprised and shocked. I went to the chapel to ask my soul before Jesus if I had to escape the weight and the cross or accept it as such and nothing else. I am worried, but when I became calm I decided to accept because *non recuso laborem*."[1]

This news arrived during a very sad time for Roncalli. Bulgaria, the country of his former diplomatic post, was in the middle of bloody convulsions following the political earthquake at the end of war in eastern Europe. There had been thousands of executions for members of the Bulgarian elites: Fascists, but also for members of the bourgeoisie who

---

1. *Diaries Turkey–Greece 1940–1944*, 809 (December 6, 1944). In Latin in the original ("Non recuso laborem": I do not refuse hard work).

had cooperated with the Nazis. The Irish priest Msgr. Thomas Ryan, Roncalli's most trusted aide in Istanbul, had just been transferred to Cairo.[2] Roncalli "accepted the request for obedience" from the Vatican, and after the *agrèement* of the French government arrived on December 21 he had to scramble to reach Paris after a quick stop in Rome. The nunciature in Paris, a key diplomatic post in the future of a post-Nazi Europe, needed to be occupied with haste, before January 1, 1945, when Roncalli had to present his credentials to the provisional government of the new French Republic. Given the troubles between the Vatican and de Gaulle's liberated France, Roncalli did not conceal his worries when he gave his last homily in Istanbul.

> The obedience to the Holy Father detaches me from you, and I am entrusted to another field of work in the service of the Holy See for the interests of the church in France. . . . While it might appear natural that I turn my soul to a peaceful sunset of my humble life, enjoying for many years still the sweetness of your filial love, I am suddenly pushed toward an order of concern to me unexpected and made more delicate and formidable by the severity of today's conditions in the world. . . . My good-bye is inspired by the announcement of the Gospel of peace that the persistent clamor of war still cannot suffocate. Brothers and children: peace, peace. After a long struggle of men and peoples, now dawns a time of reconciliation.[3]

2. Thomas Ryan (1915–1983) taught English to Roncalli in Turkey and later during the pontificate, and was bishop of Clonfert (Ireland) from 1963 until 1982.

3. Angelo Giuseppe Roncalli, *Predicazione a Istanbul*, 402 (December 25, 1944).

"The Mystery Roncalli": Nuncio in France (1945–1953)

Paris was a first-rate diplomatic post, one of the most important apostolic nunciatures (if not *the* most important), but the beginning of Roncalli's ministry in the French capital was far from easy. He traveled from Istanbul to Paris via Rome on December 28–30, 1944. While in Rome, on December 29, Roncalli was in an audience with Pius XII after he had received instructions from the secretariat of state regarding the ceremony for the beginning of the new year, where he would read a formal address in the presence of the leaders of the new democratic France. Roncalli's presence in Paris avoided embarrassment for both de Gaulle and the Holy See since Roncalli, and not the Soviet ambassador, would read the opening address in front of the president of the French Republic. When Roncalli landed at the airport in Paris on December 30, nobody was there to welcome him; it was a sign of the isolation that would be part of his eight years in Paris.[4] Nevertheless this appointment went beyond his dreams: "When I think about what the Lord decided for me, it seems a like dream. I have the awareness that he has been faithful to my [episcopal] motto: *oboedientia et pax*. And here I am, suddenly transported into this place, called the most important for Vatican diplomacy. I blush for myself, I am silent, and I adore [the Lord]."[5]

Roncalli knew that his work in Paris would be different than what he had done before: "I [have] no pastoral duties, such as I had in Constantinople, but instead more widespread means of doing good to men. My work is all in the

4. *Diaries France 1945–1948*, 8 (December 30, 1944).
5. Ibid., 11 (January 1945).

cause of peace."[6] Roncalli had been sent to Paris to deal with a new, democratic French government that had no intention to turn a blind eye to those Catholic bishops who, in the region of France under the control of the puppet regime of Marechal Pétain (under indirect German rule) between June 1940 and September 1944, cut a deal with the Nazis and were loyal to the collaborationist Vichy regime. For this reason, after the liberation of France, the nuncio Valerio Valeri (1936–1944) had to leave France and Pius XII sent to Paris an almost unknown papal diplomat, Roncalli. Some said that this was to send de Gaulle a message that the threats of the *Général* were not influential on the Vatican. But this appointment was Pius XII's personal decision, and Roncalli was sent to Paris surely because he was known in Rome as a diplomat "more versed in the art of negotiation than in the showdowns."[7]

There were preconditions for this long period in Roncalli's life, a period that some (especially in France) called "the mystery Roncalli."[8] How could the former nuncio in Paris, not at ease with the pastoral innovations of French Catholicism, become the pope who called Vatican II? Others have called it "a continual pastoral visit that lasted eight years" due to Roncalli's habit of visiting dioceses and churches all over France.[9] For sure these eight years in Paris were a long transitional period before the prestigious eccle-

6. *Pope John XXIII, Letters to His Family*, trans. Dorothy White (New York/Toronto: McGraw-Hill, 1970), 495 (February 20, 1945).

7. *Diaries France 1945–1948*, introduction by Étienne Fouilloux, xi.

8. Robert Rouquette, "Le mystère Roncalli," *Études* (July 1963); 4–18.

9. Giancarlo Zizola, *The Utopia of Pope John XXIII* (Maryknoll, NY: Orbis, 1978), 87.

siastical post as cardinal of Venice first and then as pope: Roncalli's time in Paris was "between the exile in the East and the final ascent."[10] Once again, Roncalli saw this turn of events as evidence that he did not need to plan his life:

> What happened in my poor life in these three months does not cease to amaze and confound me. How many times I happen to confirm the good principle not to worry about anything, not to look for anything for my future! . . . I do not have to hide the truth from myself: I am definitely walking toward old age. The spirit reacts and protests because it feels still so young, brisk, agile, and fresh. But just one look in the mirror is enough to confound me. This is the season of maturity: I must therefore produce more and better, thinking that perhaps the time allotted to live is short, and I am already close to the gates of eternity.[11]

From a political, cultural, and ecclesiastical standpoint, Paris was not Istanbul. The challenges were different, and Roncalli was under public scrutiny more than before, with the eyes of a more sophisticated and diversified audience. France, and Paris in particular, was the center of postwar European culture, but also a secularized "pays de mission" that had been the "eldest daughter of the church" from early Christianity to the French revolution. France represented a cultural shock for Roncalli, but was a first-rate post from a political standpoint. His new diplomatic post gave him one more reason to work at his skills, something he brought up again as a pope: "My inclination to talk often pushes me to

10. Giuseppe Alberigo, *Papa Giovanni 1881–1963* (Bologna: EDB, 2000), 103.

11. Angelo Giuseppe Roncalli, *Il Giornale dell'Anima*, 384–85 (March 26–April 2, 1945).

exuberance in my verbal manifestations. Careful, careful! I must learn how to be silent, to speak with moderation, to be able to refrain from judging people and tendencies, except when this is requested by my superiors and by the grave matters involved. In all, I should say less than more, and I should be afraid of saying too much."[12]

Roncalli's disposition was especially useful for the top diplomat of the Vatican in Paris, the capital of the European country where World War II had turned into a low-intensity civil war (a fact that French culture openly recognized only much later) and where the Catholic Church had always played an important role in the cultural and social life of French history. His first and most urgent issue was the request of de Gaulle for the resignation of a long list of bishops (the longest of these lists included twenty-four names) that the "new France" determined had been too involved with former head of state Petain's regime. Roncalli managed to have only four bishops leave their dioceses, thus preserving the Catholic Church in France from a collective judicial procedure and making the church one of the many collective bodies in postwar Europe that transitioned to a new age without too much scrutiny. Roncalli convinced the four bishops to retire voluntarily, and the Vatican appointed new bishops for those dioceses. Between July and October 1945 the issue was solved in a satisfactory manner for the Vatican. In contrast to France, the events leading to the end of World War II in Italy were difficult. In his diary Roncalli wrote about the execution of Mussolini and his mistress Claretta Petacci by the partisans, the "so-called patriots," "[theirs is] a bloody and implacable gospel, but I had invoked mercy and peace."[13]

12. Ibid., 386 (March 26–April 2, 1945).
13. *Diaries France 1945–1948*, 54 (April 30, 1945).

Roncalli also found Paris to be a challenging post because, between the interwar period and the 1950s, France became the forefront of Catholic theology dealing with modernity. France was not only the cradle of the *nouvelle théologie*, but also of new pastoral experiments, such as the *pastorale d'ensemble*, the worker-priest movement, the *mission de France* and *mission de Paris*, and the missions of French Catholic scholars and priests traveling to Latin America planting seeds for what later would be known as "liberation theology." Roncalli visited the centers of this shift in theological culture (the publishing house Cerf and the seminary of Le Saulchoir in February and March of 1946), but his religious sensibility was not always comfortable with the new theological language explored by progressive French theologians.

Available sources are not definite about how Roncalli addressed these issues or what he communicated to the Vatican, but it is clear that Roncalli perceived a difference between his Tridentine theological education and background and the culture of modern French Catholicism. In 1947 he received a visit from Jacques Maritain, and Roncalli saw that he also worried about "the intellectual extravagances that trouble the clergy in France."[14] A few weeks later he read with pleasure an essay by Jesuit Guy de Broglie about "the reveries of the modern reformers of theology."[15] Roncalli also was not impressed by the Dominican Marie-Dominique Chenu (one of the key theologians for the "new theology" and later for Vatican II) when he listened to him speak in October 1948, but he read *Vraie et fausse réforme dans l'Église* by Yves Congar, one of the most consequential

14. Ibid., 324 (May 17, 1947).
15. Ibid., 332 (June 12, 1947).

theological books of the twentieth-century for understanding the place of reform in the life of the Church.[16]
Roncalli invited many French Catholics to the residence of
the nuncio, but nobody from the milieu of liberal French
Catholic theologians (with the exception of the Abbè Pierre,
whom Roncalli perceived as a very odd priest).[17] In the
spiritual exercises of December 1947 he had already expressed his conflicted spirit about French Catholicism:

> In my conscience I feel a contrast, which sometimes be-
> comes a scruple, among the praise that I would like to
> tribute to these brave and dear Catholics of France, and
> the imperative duty to refuse to conceal politeness or fear
> of displeasing, whether out of the limitations and the true
> state of the eldest daughter (French Catholicism) of the
> church in her religious practice, the discomfort for the
> unresolved school issue, the failure of the clergy, the spread
> of secularism and communism. . . . This implies a contin-
> ued vigilance in my verbal expressions—a sweet silence
> without harshness: benevolent words, inspired by mercy
> and indulgence, will make more good than statements
> made in confidence.[18]

Roncalli repeated these words about the limits and exuber-
ances of French Catholicism and the need for him to be
cautious and merciful in 1952,[19] a few months before leav-

---

16. Alberto Melloni, *Papa Giovanni. Un cristiano e il suo concilio*
(Turin: Einaudi, 2009), 124.

17. Étienne Fouilloux, "Le nonce Roncalli et l'Église de France,"
in *L'ora che sta il mondo attraversando. Giovanni XXIII di fronte
alla storia*, eds. Giovanni Grado Merlo and Francesco Mores (Rome:
Edizioni di Storia e Letteratura, 2009), 213–26.

18. Roncalli, *Il Giornale dell'Anima*, 392–93 (December 8–13,
1947).

19. Ibid., 408 (April 10–12, 1952).

ing France. While in France Roncalli explored French Catholicism, but his impressions were not very different from the beginning of his mission in Paris. The nuncio traveled extensively (forty-eight times between 1945 and 1948), but mostly in countryside churches and sanctuaries so he did not become familiar with Catholicism being inculturated by urban settings. He preferred churches and monasteries that did not experiment with the liturgy, because he did not always approve of liturgical innovations.[20] He also was sometimes critical of innovations in sacred architecture. He called the Matisse chapel of the Dominican Sisters in Vence (in southern France) "truly an essay in authentic perversion of the artistic and liturgical taste."[21]

As in Bulgaria and in Turkey, the diplomatic post in Paris was a window for Roncalli's explorations of the world. He visited Algeria, Corsica, Tunisia, and Morocco, and spent his summer vacations in his native town. In 1950, the year of jubilee (the jubilee of the church proclaimed by Pius XII and 25 years of episcopate of Roncalli), the apostolic nuncio to Paris was on the road 151 days, including visits to the Netherlands, Belgium, and Spain.[22] These travels were possible because the years during the second part of Roncalli's mission to France, after 1948, were less difficult than the first four years. The year 1950 was important because of Pius XII's encyclical *Humani Generis* (August 12, 1950)

---

20. See, for example, *Diaries France 1949–1953*, 458 (December 2, 1951).

21. *Diaries France 1949–1953*, 435 (October 1, 1951). It is not about French Catholicism, for example, on April 18, 1919, when Roncalli said of his fellow Catholics from Bergamo: "When it comes to sacred music, my fellow *Bergamaschi* reveal themselves as real *idioti*" (in *Diaries 1905–1925*, 414).

22. *Diaries France 1949–1953*, 155.

against the "new theology." This encyclical hit French theologians particularly hard, and many of them were silenced and marginalized until Vatican II, when they became the important theologians of the council, thanks to the new pope, Roncalli—John XXIII. Since Roncalli was out of France most of 1950, it was hard to know his level of awareness of the very serious consequences of *Humani Generis* in the country. But on December 20, 1950, Roncalli wrote harsh words against the critics of *Humani Generis* in his journal: "How ridiculous the arrogance of these youth scientists, who still have milk to their mouth, and judge [the encyclical] without judgment nor foundation. For them the church does not matter: it is the science that matters."[23]

Roncalli also had a lengthy visit to Algeria (considered part of the French territory, not a colony) in 1950, well before Algeria became a war theater for the dying French colonialism. Roncalli was seen by many French Catholics to have embarrassing friends among French conservatives and reactionaries, but Roncalli was not a nationalist, and French nationalists were relieved (as well as many other French politicians, theologians, and church leaders) when he left France to become Patriarch of Venice. Roncalli was not at ease with many aspects of post-World War II France. His discomfort was more visible around theological issues, such as the scandal caused by the publication of a kind of "Catholic *art of love*" book in 1950; Roncalli called this pastoral experiment in Catholic teaching of sexual morality "unspeakable recklessness."[24] It was the same discomfort he suffered with the experience of the worker-priests. After

23. Ibid., 307 (December 20, 1950).
24. Ibid., 168 (January 22, 1950). The book had been withdrawn from bookstores already in August 1950 upon order of the Holy Office.

a meeting with Catholic nuns in June 1951, he compared them to the priests living their sacerdotal calling in the factories among workers, and he did not approve of them in light of his Tridentine formation: "The worker-priests more than ever appear in contrast to the priestly spirit. Now the Holy See will act with proper measures and I doubt they will be able to comply."[25] But as a historian, Roncalli knew that the energetic spirit of French Catholicism had always been part of the church, and patience was needed.[26] After leaving France he made it clear that he had nothing to do with the Vatican dispositions against the worker-priests that had been issued in January 1954.[27]

Roncalli was not always pleased with the church in France, but Rome was not always pleased with Roncalli—the nuncio traveled extensively, but did not always submit his reports on time (a problem of which the nuncio was aware). It is clear that Roncalli was not a typical Vatican diplomat, even in a primary diplomatic post such as Paris for the Holy See. He spent more time in pastoral activities as a man of the church in France than in touch with French politicians and other diplomats. The quality of the bishops appointed in France during Roncalli's tenure as nuncio (bishops liked by Rome more than by French Catholics) did not say much about Roncalli.[28] Roncalli read a lot, but more history and literature than philosophy and the new theology that was written and published in France in the two decades before World War II and after. This new theology was a strong trend in French Catholic theology, and Roncalli was

25. *Diaries France 1949–1953*, 396 (June 28, 1951).
26. Ibid., 517 (March 29, 1952).
27. Ibid., xii.
28. Ibid., xiii.

not part of this milieu while in France or even when he became a cardinal. With Roncalli there was "no culture of the cliques, parties, lobbying groups . . . he refuses to build his own spiritual or ideological foyer."[29]

Roncalli's time in Paris was more valuable to him for his look at the world rather than at French Catholicism *per se*. Participation in the peace conference of 1946 and the general assemblies of UNESCO in 1948 and 1951 (especially in 1951 when he was appointed observer for the Holy See to UNESCO) allowed Roncalli to acquire experience in international affairs that would bear fruits for the role of the Vatican in the *Ostpolitik* at the height of the Cold War. On November 25, 1952, he hosted a reception at the nunciature for the participants of the UNESCO conference: "350 people of different religions and ideologies, coming from all over the world. To give tribute to the apostolic nuncio is to give tribute to the pope. . . . The reception was successful; it seems that it made a special and good impression on the Protestants."[30]

Bible, Liturgy, and Ecumenism: Patriarch of Venice (1953–1958)

On November 14, 1952, the day before his one hundreth trip as nuncio in France, Roncalli received a confidential letter from the Secretariat of State (via then-Msgr. Montini, later Pope Paul VI) on behalf of Pius XII. The Vatican asked Roncalli about his availability for the appointment to patriarch of Venice, because the sitting patriarch, Carlo Agos-

29. Alberto Melloni, "Formazione e sviluppo della cultura di Roncalli," *Papa Giovanni*, ed. Giuseppe Alberigo (Rome/Bari: Laterza, 1987), 19.

30. *Diaries France 1949–1953*, 621 (November 25–26, 1952).

tini, was seriously ill (he died at the end of the month). Roncalli's reaction was of surprise and obedience: "*Oboedientia et pax . . .* this is an unexpected diversion on the directions of my life."[31] On November 29 Roncalli received the official confirmation of his appointment as a cardinal that would be made by Pius XII in the consistory on January 12, 1953. He was one of the new (and very few) cardinals of Pius XII. Roncalli wrote, "I am not surprised, but I am glad to not feel any personal glorification or sense of vain glory, or otherwise. Everything happens according to obedience and abandonment to the will of the Lord. Among the cardinals there were scoundrels and saints: I want to be among them *in humilitate: in simplicitate: in amore Dei et animarum in decore S. Ecclesiae.*"[32]

Roncalli saw the appointment as the accomplishment of his life in the church, not because he was becoming a cardinal, but because he could be a bishop taking care of souls:

> It is interesting that divine providence takes me now where my priestly vocation took me, that is, the pastoral ministry. Now I am in full, direct ministry of souls. In truth, I have always believed that for a man of the church the so-called ecclesiastical diplomacy must be imbued with pastoral spirit, otherwise it counts for nothing and turns to ridicule a holy mission. I am now placed before the true good of souls and of the church in relation to its purpose, that is, to save souls to lead them to heaven.[33]

Roncalli had been away from his own country since 1924, for almost thirty years, in a completely different political, cultural, and social situation than the one in Italy. In the

31. Ibid., 616 (November 14, 1952).
32. Ibid., 622 (November 29, 1952).
33. Roncalli, *Il Giornale dell'Anima,* 412 (May 1953).

1950s postwar Italy was still recovering from the destruction of World War II, and the Catholic Church was very powerful in the political realm, which was different from all the countries where Roncalli had previously served. The pivotal party was the Christian-Democratic Party (Democrazia Cristiana), and in the spring of 1953 when Roncalli arrived in Venice, Italy was full of tension because of a new electoral law that the Christian-Democratic Party unsuccessfully tried to pass to its own advantage. The country was politically divided between the "Catholic party" and the two parties of Socialists and Communists. Much of the public activity of the Catholic Church in Italy was well-disciplined but clearly aimed at maintaining the power of the Christian-Democratic Party to avoid a Marxist takeover of the country and deter cooperation between Catholics and Socialists-Communists both at the national and local level. Regarding the church, Roncalli's time in Venice coincided with the long and dramatic end of the pontificate of Pius XII. The pope died in October 1958, but his health had been seriously compromised since 1954.[34]

Roncalli arrived in Venice on March 15, 1953 (only a few days after Stalin's death). At age seventy-one he was significantly older than his predecessors at the beginning of their ministry as patriarchs. Roncalli felt that he was entering the final years of his life. Three of his sisters (Ancilla, Teresa, and Maria) had died between 1953 and 1955; his brother Giovanni died in 1956. He introduced himself to the Venetians in a humble, non-rhetorical, and genuinely autobiographical way:

34. *Diaries Venice 1953–1955*, 216 (February 7, 1954).

You have waited for me anxiously, and people have said and written of me things that far surpass my merits. I humbly introduce myself. Like every other man who lives down here [on earth]: I live with the grace of good physical health, with a little common sense for me to see things early and clear, with a disposition for the love of others that keeps me faithful to the law of the Gospel, with respect of my right and the right of others that prevent me from hurting anyone: all this encourages me to do good to all. I come from a humble background and was educated in blessed poverty, which has few needs, protects the flourishing of the noblest and highest virtues, and prepares the high ascents of life. Providence brought me forth from my native village and made me walk the streets of the world in the East and in the West, approaching people of different religions and ideologies; put me in contact with acute and threatening social problems, and kept within me the sense of calm, balanced inquiry, and appreciation of things. I have always been focused more on what unites than on what separates and elicits contrasts among us, with all due respect to the principles of the Catholic faith and morals.[35]

Roncalli was comfortable with the poverty of his family background—"I was educated in blessed poverty,"[36] he wrote—but he was not pleased with the poor finances of the diocese of Venice, which limited the ability of his actions. He wanted to be a bishop whose actions were inspired by "humility, simple adherence *verbo et opere* to the Gospel, fearless meekness, unbeatable patience, fatherly and

35. First speech of Patriarch Roncalli in the Cathedral of St. Mark, March 15, 1953, quoted by Enrico Galavotti in the introduction of *Diaries Venice 1953–1955*, vii.

36. Roncalli, *Il Giornale dell'Anima*, 414 (May 1953).

insatiable zeal."[37] He wanted to lead his church with "vigilant, patient, and enduring goodness, and not with the whip."[38] A few months after his arrival in Venice he wrote in his journal, "I did not deserve anything; I did not aspire to anything; but everything was given to me."[39]

Venice was not typical of a diocese governed by a cardinal. It was prestigious but was not considered as important as the ecclesiastical sees like Milan or Paris or Madrid. However, it was not a small diocese. Roncalli's flock numbered 360,000 faithful, 100 parishes, 241 diocesan priests, 301 priests of religious orders, and 30 seminarians.[40] Venice had the typical problems of a normal Italian and European diocese in the twentieth century: a declining number of priestly vocations (it was happening already in the 1950s), the structure and location of the seminary (geographically distant from the city of Venice), a clergy at times problematic to govern, and the difficulty of creating a team of people with whom to work effectively. Roncalli chose Loris Francesco Capovilla as his secretary (who also would become Roncalli's secretary after he was elected pope). Venice was also an ancient city with a growing population of workers in the outskirts of the city on the *terra ferma*, thanks to new government-subsidized chemical plants; Roncalli had to create new parishes and adapt the ecclesiastical structures to the changing social reality of northern Italy becoming fully industrialized. On May 1, 1954, in the industrial district of Marghera, the patriarch of Venice inaugurated the "Jesus the Worker" parish—the first in Italy with this

37. Ibid., 415 (May 1953).
38. Ibid., 423 (May 1955).
39. *Diaries Venice 1953–1955*, 98 (July 11, 1953).
40. Ibid., 4.

name.[41] In the short speech given for the occasion, the patriarch said, "I remember here my father, head of a very large family. . . . It is not humiliating for me to tell you that all my brothers are workers, I was born in a family of workers."[42]

Roncalli was a member of the Italian bishops' conference, which at that time did not exist officially and gathered only the metropolitan archbishops of the ecclesiastical regions in the Italian peninsula. The meetings of this conference of Italian bishops were a prelude to the formation of the "Conferenza Episcopale Italiana" at Vatican II. Roncalli took part in the meetings, having in mind the more structured conference of the French bishops that he experienced when he was nuncio in Paris. During this time, Roncalli became more known in the Italian church beyond his reputation in the Vatican circles of the Roman Curia and in the diplomatic milieu.

As a bishop, Roncalli did not develop a pastoral plan, but clearly had in mind priorities for the Christian formation of his church: Scripture, liturgy, and ecumenism. The first year (1954) of the new patriarch's time in Venice was also the year of the canonization of Pius X, the pope of the anti-modernist purge and a former patriarch of Venice (1894–1903). Roncalli, who had met Pius X in Rome immediately after his ordination in 1904, prepared the diocese of Venice for the event. The year 1954 was important for Roncalli for other reasons, too. In January during the week of prayer for Christian unity, Roncalli organized the liturgical celebrations for the week and was personally active in three public

41. Ibid., 264 (May 1, 1954).
42. Angelo Giuseppe Roncalli, *Scritti e discorsi*, vol. I, 1953–1954 (Rome: Paoline, 1959), 204.

lectures on the history of different Christian traditions. Due to his personal experience in eastern Europe with his broad pastoral and ecumenical ministry in Bulgaria and Turkey, Roncalli was an absolute exception within the Italian episcopate. In October 1954, in a lecture during the international Eucharistic congress in Lebanon, Roncalli talked about ecumenism as the task of "rebuilding Catholicity in its amplitude and perfection . . . the most important event in modern times."[43] He was also critical of the excessive particularism of the eastern Catholic bishops he had met in Lebanon: "These eastern Catholics are good, good. But too much attachment to that which divides rather than that which unites."[44]

On a retreat with the clergy in September 1954, Roncalli talked about the key sources for Christian life: Scripture and Eucharist. Reading the Bible was not part of the culture of Italian Catholics, so Roncalli's comment was atypical as was his invitation to the clergy to "unite the people to the altar."[45] Roncalli had not been a member of the international network of the liturgical movement, but he had always emphasized the importance of church history in his education and the centrality of the liturgy in his spiritual life. Roncalli did not initiate the "liturgical experiments" performed and advocated by the theologians of the movement, but it was no accident in May 1959, when he was the new pope, that he "discreetly" donated five million Italian lire to the association working on the series of the fathers of the church, *Sources*

43. Giuseppe Alberigo, *Dalla laguna al Tevere. Angelo Giuseppe Roncalli da San Marco a San Pietro* (Bologna: il Mulino, 2000), 66; *Diaries Venice 1953–1955*, 369–76 (October 19–28, 1954).

44. *Diaries Venice 1953–1955*, 375 (October 27, 1954).

45. Alberigo, *Dalla laguna al Tevere*, 47–48.

Chrétiennes.[46] In 1955 there were polemics in the patriarchate because of the changes made to the internal structure of
the Basilica of San Marco in order to make the liturgy more
available to the faithful. Roncalli had no patience for the
nostalgic and the obsession with liturgical aesthetics: "Day
by day unfolds the scam that has been created by very few
people, artists who have eyes for the arts only and do not
know and do not appreciate liturgy, and ancient caryatids
of an outdated nobility, still worthy of some respect, but not
entitled to impose themselves on the common sense."[47] But
Roncalli's approach was low-key when it came to the persona of the patriarch: "I am annoyed by the ones who, for
sincere affection or for goodness's sake, insist to celebrate
my priestly jubilee in externalities that are repugnant to my
character and temperament. We must be patient."[48]

In 1955 Roncalli launched the "mission in the city" and
to lead it called Fr. Giovanni Rossi, one of the most interesting priests in Italy during the 1950s who was president of
the "Pro Civitate Christiana" in Assisi (an association of lay
and ordained Catholics founded in 1939 and engaged in
dialogue with the modern world).[49] But it was in 1956 that
the patriarch of Venice revealed more of his theology. As a
good historian, Roncalli knew how to use anniversaries to
renew the attention of his people to forgotten parts of the
Christian tradition. That year was the five-hundred-year
anniversary of the first patriarch of Venice, St. Lorenzo

---

46. Étienne Fouilloux, *La Collection "Sources chrétiennes." Editer
les Pères de l'Eglise au XXe siècle* (Paris: Cerf, 1995), 219.

47. *Diaries Venice 1953–1955*, 535 (June 30, 1955).

48. Ibid., 302–3 (July 3, 1954).

49. See Massimo Toschi, *Per la Chiesa e per gli uomini. Don
Giovanni Rossi (1887–1975)* (Genoa: Marietti, 1990).

Giustiniani (1381–1456), and in the diocesan bulletin Roncalli published the article "Guidelines for Reading the Holy Book" (*Norme pratiche per la lettura e lo studio del libro sacro*), with detailed advice for a closer contact with the Bible. The role of the Bible was "perhaps the only difference between the spiritual life of Roncalli and the traditional features of Catholic piety at the beginning of the twentieth century."[50] He carried that practice with him for his whole life, even when he became bishop and later pope. Biblical literacy in Italy had been minimal since the Council of Trent and the Counter-Reformation, when Catholic bishops and clergy sometimes organized bonfires of Bibles to make an anti-Protestant statement both to their flock and to the inquisitors coming from Rome.[51] In post-Trent Italy, the Bible was reserved for those who knew Latin, and only the Latin version of the *Vulgate* was permitted; this culture was still alive in many bishops until Vatican II. Roncalli was educated in the tradition of Trent, but was original in his thoughts about Catholic leadership of pre-Vatican II Italy. On February 15, 1956, Roncalli published a pastoral letter, "Sacred Scripture and St. Lorenzo Giustiniani." The most important public statements of Roncalli during 1956 were about the Bible. His work for the pastoral letter was also the occasion for the patriarch to renew his love also for the fathers of the church, like Ephrem the Syrian.[52] In 1956, a politically tense year for Italy, Roncalli, the cardinal patriarch of one of the political epicenters of the new political balance of power in

50. Alberigo, *Papa Giovanni*, 123.
51. See Gigliola Fragnito, *La Bibbia al rogo. La censura ecclesiastica e i volgarizzamenti della Scrittura (1471–1605)* (Bologna: il Mulino, 1997).
52. *Diaries Venice 1956–1958*, 45–46 (February 17, 1956).

the country, stayed clear of interferences with politics and went "back to the sources." His pastoral letter was "a statement about his freedom and about the message of the Gospel in a church heavily ideologized."[53]

The year 1956 was tragic for Europe with the Soviet repression of the uprising in Budapest; many refugees ended up in Venice because of its historical ties with eastern Europe.[54] Italy felt the repercussions of the Hungarian bloodbath in its domestic politics, and the Catholic Church saw the peril of communism infiltrating Italy. By 1954 Venice had already hosted priests, seminarians, religious, and nuns expelled by neighboring Yugoslavia under communist rule.[55] Roncalli was not an anticommunist propagandist like other Italian bishops, such as Girolamo Bortignon, bishop of the neighboring diocese of Padua. Roncalli did not have an optimistic view of communist and socialist ideologies, but his way to deal with communists and socialists was more dialogical and less combative. He was not a liberal bishop: in January 1957 he gave a speech on the "five wounds of a big crucifix"—liberalism, Marxism, "democratism," freemasonry, and secularism.[56] He could have used all the rhetorical tools of the anti-secularist Catholic culture, but he was not comfortable with that. In October 1956, after the Budapest uprising, he gave a strong homily denouncing the Soviet action in Hungary, but he did not like using this style: "I had to impress . . . but certainly this style does not match my ordinary habit of preaching."[57]

53. Melloni, *Papa Giovanni*, 65.
54. *Diaries Venice 1956–1958*, 263 (December 5, 1956).
55. Roncalli, *Scritti e discorsi*, 184–85.
56. *Diaries Venice 1956–1958*, 293 (January 2, 1957).
57. Ibid., 240 (October 29, 1956).

Roncalli always distinguished between "error" and "the errant." In his final encyclical, *Pacem in Terris*, he enlisted this distinction to affirm that Catholics, "in order to achieve some external good," may "collaborate . . . with those who through error lack the fullness of faith in Christ" (PT 158). It was in this context that he invited the Venetians to welcome the delegates of the Italian Socialist Party to hold their convention in the city in 1957.[58] This message caused some uproar and scandal among Catholics used to treating Socialists with contempt. On one hand Roncalli did not want to be the exception of the Italian bishops' loyalty to the strict directives of the Holy Office of Cardinal Alfredo Ottaviani about the cooperation with Marxists in Italian politics. Roncalli was in constant touch with the Vatican about these issues between 1955 and 1956, and he had not made waves: "In the afternoon I prepared my message concerning the upcoming political elections. I remained faithful to my disposition, even if I said everything in accordance with Rome's instructions: and I am glad of that."[59]

On the other hand Roncalli's refusal to condemn those who sought more cooperation between Catholics and Socialists in Italy (and in Venice specifically, with the Christian-Democrats gathered around young Wladimiro Dorigo, seen as a leftist by mainstream Catholics) brought him criticisms within the Catholic hierarchy and especially among the bishops of the Veneto region.[60] They did not understand why the patriarch of Venice did not condemn the new city administration, which was formed in July 1956 by the Christian-Democratic Party with the external support of the Socialists.

58. Giancarlo Zizola, *The Utopia of Pope John XXIII* (Maryknoll, NY: Orbis Books, 1978), 219–22.

59. *Diaries Venice 1953–1955*, 71 (May 19, 1953).

60. Zizola, *The Utopia of Pope John XXIII*, 209–19.

Roncalli supported the Christian-Democratic Party and its proximity to the Catholic Church, and rejected Marxist ideologies, but his pastoral touch prevailed: "It is a person who comes to the confessional presence, not the political party or the ideology. This person is entrusted to our catechesis, our love, and our pastoral creativity. This requires a case-by-case basis, with extreme caution. If you impose something drastically, he will not understand you or will understand the opposite; if you reject him, he will be gone and will not come back."[61] On another occasion, in May 1956 when commenting on the document of the Holy Office about Italian politics, Roncalli explained succinctly his view of the role of the church: "It is the Lord who creates the minds, and it is the Lord who can fix them with his grace."[62]

It is striking that the messages from Roncalli differ not in substance but in style with the messages coming from the Vatican, which was vocally opposed to any *détente* with Socialists in Italian politics. Roncalli was in favor of a continuing Christian-Democratic hegemony on Italy, but he always avoided the tactics of the anticommunist crusaders in 1950s Italy: "I can see that my spiritual temperament does not agree with some of my brothers, for example, [the bishops of] Vicenza, Padova, Chioggia *on this point* in the *way of saying* the most serious and difficult things, so as not to irritate, and to let people reflect."[63] But Roncalli was not only about caution and style when it came to Italian history and politics. On February 11, 1954, he gave a speech for the twenty-fifth anniversary of the "peace" between Italy

61. Angelo Giuseppe Roncalli, *Questo è il mistero della mia vita*, vol. I, ed. Loris Francesco Capovilla (Bergamo 1990), 23, quoted by Enrico Galavotti in *Diaries Venice 1956–1958*, xiii.

62. *Diaries Venice 1956–1958*, 124 (May 25, 1956).

63. Ibid., 646 (December 14, 1955).

and the Vatican, in which he said that Mussolini played a "providential" role (an expression coined by Pius XI).[64] He was able to navigate perilous waters. The issue of the "conciliazione," that is, the solution of the "Roman question" between the church and the Fascist regime in 1929, was still taboo for everybody in 1950s Italy (also for the Communists, who accepted the provisions of the Fascist Concordat of 1929 as part of the new constitution promulgated in 1947).

In Venice Roncalli was in touch with the new elite of Italian tycoons (the Cini family donated generously to the initiatives of the diocese), with many other bishops and cardinals (he received the visits of American cardinals in pilgrimage in Italy), and with the world of modern art and culture (at the Venice Biennale for the arts he met with Igor Stravinsky for a Mass for St. Mark in August 1956).[65] Previously though, in 1954, he warned the lay people of Venice and prohibited clergy and members of religious orders to visit the "Biennale d'arte" because of the scandalous works of art exhibited there. The letter was dated June 21, 1954, which was the feast of St. Aloysius Gonzaga, the pubescent saint, model of perfect purity.[66]

The episcopal ministry for the diocese of Venice occupied much of Roncalli's time, and sometimes he accomplished his work using unusual or almost forgotten ways of governing the local church, such as the diocesan synod. Venice celebrated one in 1957, the year Roncalli could first appoint a new vicar general. A diocesan synod was one of the institutions recommended by the Council of Trent for the govern-

64. Ibid., 219 (February 11, 1954). For the text of his lecture, see Roncalli, *Scritti e discorsi*, vol. I, 1953–1954, 160–70.

65. *Diaries Venice 1956–1958*, 180–81 (August 10, 1956).

66. Roncalli, *Scritti e discorsi*, vol. I, 1953–1954, 234–35.

ment of dioceses, but between the seventeenth and early twentieth centuries the diocesan synod as an institution had gone through a significant period of oblivion, not only in Italy. The last diocesan synod for Venice had been celebrated in 1926, more than thirty years before. It was not a coincidence that the patriarch of Venice, the historian of Trent, concluded his work in Venice in 1957 on his history of St. Charles Borromeo's pastoral visits to Bergamo.[67]

Roncalli saw himself concluding his work life in Venice. For the first time he declined (but always through an appropriate use of carefully-worded language) the possibility of becoming secretary of the Concistorial Congregation of the Roman Curia, replacing cardinal Adeodato Piazza, his predecessor in Venice between 1936 and 1948, who died in November 1957. In his letter of December 6, 1957, for the first time Roncalli said "no" to Rome. He said he was already seventy-seven years old, and that he remembered the value of the old saying *nosce teipsum*—"you must know yourself."[68] This was just one of the many interesting turns in the relationship between Roncalli and the Roman Curia, from the tensions of the 1920s and 1930s to the invitation to become part of it as a cardinal in 1957. Roncalli showed that he could stand up to the Roman congregations in 1958, when he defended the bishop of Lourdes, Pierre-Marie Théas, who had been accused by the Roman Curia of

67. See *Gli atti della visita apostolica di S. Carlo Borromeo a Bergamo*, 5 volumes, ed. Angelo Giuseppe Roncalli (Florence: Olschki, 1936–1958).

68. Letter published in Marco Roncalli, *Giovanni XXIII. Nel ricordo del segretario Loris F. Capovilla* (Cinisello Balsamo: San Paolo, 1995) 226–27, and reproduced by Galavotti in *Diaries Venice 1956–1958*, 532–33.

corruption. Roncalli knew Théas since the time he was nuncio in Paris and did not mind positioning himself against the Curia machine. Roncalli's action helped the bishop of Lourdes resist the attacks.

At the beginning of 1958, Cardinal Roncalli seemed very far from Rome, psychologically and "politically." His spiritual exercises of July 1958 were focused on "interior peace."[69] In September 1958, a few weeks before the death of Pius XII and the conclave that would elect him pope, he wrote in his journal, "My advanced age should make myself more cautious in accepting preaching engagements outside of my diocese. I have to write everything down and this costs me, in addition to the constant humiliation that I feel for my own paucity. The Lord help me and forgive me."[70]

But, at the beginning of October, as the health of Pius XII was rapidly deteriorating, Roncalli left in his diaries some signals—without clarifying much—that in the future he might be called to some higher office in Rome.[71]

69. Roncalli, *Il Giornale dell'Anima*, 432–41 (July 9–13, 1958).
70. Ibid., 444–45 (September 22–26, 1958).
71. *Diaries Venice 1956–1958*, 742 (October 6, 1958).

CHAPTER FIVE

A Pope of Temporary Transition with a Robust Program: Rome

(1958–1963)

Defying Expectations: Conclave, Election, and Inception

Pius XII died on October 9, 1958, and for the Catholic Church it was the end of an age. The conclave of October 1958 was essentially an open conclave with no natural candidate to succeed Eugenio Pacelli. Pacelli had governed the church for almost two decades as a pope, but even longer considering his years as the top diplomat of the Vatican in the tumultuous times before becoming pope. The electoral College of Cardinals in 1958 was a relatively small one. There were fifty-one cardinals; eighteen of them, more than one-third, were Italian. As always, diplomats in Rome from all over the world were focused on the Catholic Church in this crucial moment and tried to predict who the new pope would be. Roncalli's name came up in one of the pre-conclave diplomatic reports, the one drafted by the Italian ambassador to the Holy See, Francesco Giorgio Mameli, who already in 1954 (when Pius XII became seriously ill) saw in Roncalli the perfect candidate in terms of age, curriculum, pastoral touch, and—of course—nationality.[1]

But in 1958 Roncalli was not a natural candidate. There were competitors, like the Armenian (but technically a Soviet citizen who had been in the Roman Curia for a long time) Cardinal Grégoire-Pierre Agagianian and the camerlengo (chamberlain) of the Holy Roman Church, Cardinal Benedetto Aloisi Masella. But Roncalli knew that he was one of the candidates. From Rome he wrote to his niece about what the Roncalli family was reading in the press about the conclave: "Dear Enrica, just a few lines to tell you and all our relations that I am well and in good spirits, and you all must not believe the gossip of the newspapers. These will be days of mystery for me and for many, in fact for all the cardinals."[2] But in the days immediately preceding the conclave, Roncalli had many meetings with other cardinals and members of the Roman Curia, and between October 15 and 18 he perceived that he was a candidate in the eyes of many.[3] On October 26 he decided to have dinner in his room, in order

---

1. Alberto Melloni, *L'altra Roma. Politica e S. Sede durante il concilio Vaticano II (1959–1965)* (Bologna: il Mulino, 2000), 33–35.

2. *Pope John XXIII, Letters to His Family*, trans. Dorothy White (New York/Toronto: McGraw-Hill, 1970), 818 (October 20, 1958). The diaries for the days of the conclave report the fact that Roncalli met with other cardinals and heads of Roman dicasteries, but nothing about the content of these meetings. The lack of details in the letters to his family has also to do with the fact that these letters were likely to be read in public.

3. *Diaries Venice 1956–1958*, 753–56.

to let the other cardinals talk about him. But the night before the decisive vote, on October 27, he returned to the dinner table with the other cardinals; he did not want to send a message about his aspirations to the papacy.[4] On October 28, 1958, after the tenth vote, he went to his room for a solitary lunch, just before the eleventh and final vote.

Roncalli's election was the outcome of a short conclave, just three days and eleven votations; he received either thirty-six or thirty-eight votes out of fifty, one or three more than the minimum required.[5] The runner-up was the Armenian cardinal Agagianian. Roncalli had become aware during the days before the conclave that he was seen by many as the perfect "transitional pope"—seventy-seven-years of age with a long career in the diplomatic service; Italian, but spent thirty years of his life abroad; not a member of the Roman Curia and not always in a good relationship with Rome during his career. He chose the name of John, although he knew there had been a pope John XXIII (an antipope, 1410–1415, during the western Schism). Roncalli chose the name John because it was the name of his father, of the patron saint of his birthplace, of the Baptist, and of the evangelist of charity. It was a surprise that the new pope did not choose the name of one his predecessors: Pius, Leo, or Benedict.

After the long and dramatic pontificate of Pius XII, the Catholic Church was still very powerful, but damaged internally in its ability to deal with modernity by the theological purge of 1950 and with the global threat of communism. It had serious problems in its administration, and the Roman Curia felt it needed a period of transition.

---

4. Ibid., 765–67.
5. With the records classified, the official number of votes may never be determined. See *Diaries Venice 1956–1958*, 769n817.

Many saw Roncalli as a transitional pope, of which the newly elected John XXIII was aware. Roncalli wrote about his election three years later: "On October 28, 1958, when the cardinals of the Holy Roman Church chose me to the supreme responsibility of the government of the universal flock of Jesus Christ, at seventy-seven years of age, the belief spread that I was a pope of a temporary transition. Instead I am on the eve of the fourth year of my pontificate with the vision of a robust program to be carried out with the whole world watching and waiting."[6]

As a pope of transition, Roncalli had a remarkably "robust program" indeed. In a few weeks everybody—in the Roman Curia, in the world church, in world politics, and in Italy—noticed. It was the beginning of a pontificate marked by clear resistance from some quarters of the Roman Curia, namely the Holy Office led by Cardinal Alfredo Ottaviani, against the novelties of the pontificate. This beginning was marked by the need to restore some normalcy to the institutions of the Roman Curia. First, Roncalli appointed Domenico Tardini as Secretary of State (a post left vacant since 1944), even though Tardini had been one of the most outspoken critics of Roncalli when he was a diplomat in Turkey.[7] Second, he created new cardinals in order to replenish a depleted College of Cardinals. (In his very long pontificate, Pius XII convened only two consistories, in 1946 and 1953, and created only 56 cardinals.) On December 15, 1958, John XXIII created twenty-three new cardinals, knowing that the Catholic Church had become a global church:

6. Roncalli, *Il Giornale dell'Anima*, 458 (August 10, 1961).
7. Giuseppe Alberigo, *Dalla laguna al Tevere. Angelo Giuseppe Roncalli da San Marco a San Pietro* (Bologna: il Mulino, 2000), 100.

> We start with the most important business. First, the con-
> sistory and the appointment of new cardinals. . . . We
> begin a litany, and here we [with Secretary of State Tardini]
> are in complete agreement. When we arrived at seventy
> cardinals, counting both the old and new cardinals, we
> stopped for a moment, but then we realized that at the
> time of Sixtus V, the Catholic Church occupied only a third
> of the current regions and therefore we continued and we
> appointed twenty-three new cardinals.[8]

John XXIII took other measures that restored the traditional
role of the pope as bishop of Rome, an ecclesiological element long forgotten and overshadowed by the imperial
features of the papacy. On November 23, 1958, John XXIII
took possession of the Basilica of St. John Lateran and called
that day "one of the most beautiful days in my life."[9] He
gave new solemnity to this fundamental ecclesiological and
liturgical moment in the life of the church of Rome and of
the pope as its bishop, and gave a homily that focused on
the two main sources for the spiritual life of the Christian:
the Scripture and the Eucharist.[10]

    John XXIII preached as a bishop and as a pastor. The new
pastoral touch of Pope John XXIII was visible in the first
few weeks of his pontificate with his visit to the children's
hospital and especially his visit on December 26, 1958, to

8. *Diaries Pontificate 1958–1963*, 6 (October 30, 1958). Among
the new cardinals there is also the archbishop of Milan, Giovanni
Battista Montini, who later became Roncalli's successor on June 21,
1963, as Paul VI.

    9. Ibid., 7 (November 23, 1958).

    10. Angelo Giuseppe Roncalli, *Discorsi, Messaggi, Colloqui 1958–
1963* (Vatican City: Tipografia Editrice Vaticana, 1960–1967) vol. 1,
35–47.

the prison in Rome, a few blocks from the Vatican. Before John XXIII, the previous most recent visit of a pope to the prison Regina Coeli in Rome had occurred eighty-eight years prior. During his visit Pope John XXIII gave his first great impromptu speech, in which he dared to call the prison "here, in the Father's house." In his diary John XXIII wrote about that day: "Today was my visit to the prison Regina Coeli. I kept calm by my side, but there was great admiration for my visit among Romans, Italians, and of the whole world. The pressure was great all around me. . . . These are the consolations of the pope: the exercise of fourteen works of mercy."[11]

John XXIII was enormously popular already two months after his election, at the end of 1958, because he interpreted the aspirations not only of the church, but also of the world outside. On December 25, 1958, he dedicated his Christmas radio message to the themes of unity and peace. The decision to call a new council for the Catholic Church was announced on January 25, 1959, at the end of the week of prayer for Christian unity and in the Basilica of St. Paul outside the Walls, dedicated to the apostle to the Gentiles. It was a definitive sign that his pontificate would be a transitional one but in a very different sense from what some of his electors thought—some of whom received the news of the new council in the Basilica of St. Paul outside the Walls in deafening silence (as the pope recalled a few years later).[12]

The pope announced that he planned not only the celebration of a new general council for the Catholic Church, but also a synod for the diocese of Rome (that had not seen one in centuries) and a new Code of Canon Law (the first one

11. *Diaries Pontificate 1958–1963*, 10.
12. Roncalli, *Discorsi, Messaggi, Colloqui*, vol. 4, 259 (May 8, 1962).

had been published when Roncalli was a young priest, in 1917). But the big news was the ecumenical council. A new council "for Christian unity" was an idea that had been discussed in Catholicism and in the Orthodox Church in the previous four decades, and Roncalli had been part of that environment and conversation. The Roman Curia was shocked, and many cardinals and bishops around the world were surprised by the announcement. Many thought that after the proclamation of papal infallibility at Council Vatican I (1870), councils were a relic of the past. Others thought it would take too much time for the church to organize a council during the pontificate of Roncalli. Some of the critics (especially in the Holy Office) actively tried to stop or slow down the preparation of the council, which would involve a consultation of all the individual bishops around the world.[13]

In his announcement of the council, John XXIII said explicitly that one of the goals of the council would be an ecumenical one in terms of a new relationship between the Roman Catholic Church and other "Christian communities."[14] From the very beginning of his pontificate, John XXIII sent signals about a different way of being pope and of looking at the future of the church.[15] The plan of the pontificate was not based on a specific theological platform, but on major ideas: unity, peace, charity, and mercy. These themes became visible in a magisterial way in the first encyclical, *Ad Petri*

13. *History of Vatican II*, vol. 1; John W. O'Malley, *What Happened at Vatican II* (Cambridge, MA: Belknap Press of Harvard University Press, 2008), 15–53.

14. In the original manuscript of John XXIII there is "churches" instead of "communities." See Alberto Melloni, *Papa Giovanni. Un cristiano e il suo concilio* (Torino: Einaudi, 2009), 224.

15. Melloni, *Papa Giovanni*, 207–14.

Cathedram, published on June 29, 1959. John XXIII saw in the world "the universal hope that the hearts of men would be stirred to a fuller and deeper recognition of truth, a renewal of Christian morals, and a restoration of unity, harmony, and peace."[16] John XXIII was aware that the Catholic Church was truly a global church and that the world and the church must cooperate in the effort to bring humanity to a new unity. "Roncalli's life was a quest for unity aimed at overcoming a culture of hostility that had 'others as adversaries'—a culture of unfriendliness that saw nineteenth and early twentieth-century Catholic culture as father and teacher."[17] Roncalli belonged to the generation that experienced World War I and World War II; he interpreted the renewed need for unity in a globalized but also fragmented world as a "sign of our times" that had spiritual and theological implications.

John XXIII did not neglect Italy (in October 1959 he approved the new statutes for the newly formed Italian bishops conference), but Roncalli's view was global. During those years of the Cold War and of the arms race, John XXIII saw himself as an instrument of peace. He knew that might lead to misunderstandings or risks of being used by the Kremlin-inspired ideologues of one-sided pacifism, but he was willing to do the unprecedented: "Yesterday the cardinal secretary of state spoke to me of the possible visit to the Vatican by President Eisenhower of the United States and my visit to the White House. Everything for peace in the world. My thoughts are simple: I do not want and do not aspire to

16. John XXIII, *Ad Petri Cathedram* (encyclical), June 29, 1959, par. 3.

17. Melloni, *Papa Giovanni*, 163.

anything, neither about going nor about not going."[18] Pope John received president Eisenhower in the Vatican on December 6, 1959.[19]

This global and universal view of Pope John XXIII grew from his experience as a diplomat and his education as a historian, but it was also fruit of a deeply spiritual experience. During his meals in the retreat of November 29–December 5, 1959, he had his secretary, Msgr. Capovilla, read him pages from the *De consideratione* of St. Bernard of Clairvaux, a treatise-advice addressed to Pope Eugenius III (1145–1153). In the notes taken during those spiritual exercises in Advent of 1959, Roncalli talked about his "sentiment of universality": "Since the Lord wanted me, miserable as I am, in this great service, I do not feel any belonging to something particular in life: family, fatherland, nation, particular orientations in the field of my research, and my plans."[20] As a pope, Roncalli drew inspiration from his experiences in the east and west of Europe, but he also stayed faithful to the spiritual literature of his youth, especially Thomas à Kempis that he continued to read: "Tonight, while reading chapter 50 of *The Imitation of Christ*, the third book, I had a heavenly revelation about the fact that the Lord can dispose of my poor life, for my final sanctification, and for my eternal happiness."[21]

18. *Diaries Pontificate 1958–1963*, 47–48 (September 8, 1959).

19. John XXIII had scheduled a visit of President Kennedy to the Vatican for June 1963, but the visit was cancelled by the Vatican a few days before the pope's death. See Massimo Franco, *Parallel Empires: The Vatican and the United States. Two Centuries of Alliance and Conflict* (New York: Doubleday, 2009).

20. Roncalli, *Il Giornale dell'Anima*, 449 (November 29–December 5, 1959).

21. *Diaries Pontificate 1958–1963*, 380 (May 6, 1962).

John XXIII's Church: *Aggiornamento*, Global Church, World Peace

John XXIII quickly became known as *il papa buono*, the "good pope," because of the difference in style with his predecessors. But this name risks emphasizing his *bonhomie* more than his prophetic insights. The linchpin of John XXIII's pontificate as well as his life was his decision to call a new council for the Catholic Church. It is telling that Pope John XXIII called a new council to address issues in a church that had lost touch with the conciliar tradition as a way to make decisions. John XXIII was not the first pope of the twentieth century who had this idea. Previously Pius XI in 1923 and Pius XII in 1948 explored the option to call a council, but John XXIII was the only one not afraid of the institutional and theological complexities of a council for the global Catholic Church. This decision was his; he did not start a consultation within the Roman Curia, but he informed and consulted with the Secretary of State Cardinal Tardini "out of respect for his idea of the physiology of the Roman Curia."[22] This action revealed the complexities of the pope's persona: theologically and historically faithful to the ancient conciliar tradition of the church, but also aware that some decisions had to be made by the pope personally. In this sense, Cardinal Lercaro of Bologna captured one of the key elements of Pope John XXIII's pontificate when he spoke, a few months after the pope's death, of the "institutional loneliness" of the pope of Vatican II.[23]

22. Melloni, *Papa Giovanni*, 23; *Diaries Pontificate*, 23–25 (January 15–20, 1959).

23. This interpretation of Roncalli's pontificate as "institutional loneliness" of John XXIII was advanced by the Italian and "Bolog-

John XXIII made the decision to call a council in a church that dreamed and needed it, but in a Roman Curia mostly opposed to the idea—the same Roman Curia he had to work with for the preparation of the council. In May 1959 he created for the council an "ante-preparatory commission" made of Roman Curia members and presided over by the cardinal secretary of state. The ante-preparatory period lasted one year, and it was only in the spring and summer of 1960 that the real preparation of the council began. The year 1960 opened with the celebration of the synod for the diocese of Rome decided by John XXIII. Held January 24–31, this was the first synod for the local church in modern church history. The synod was uneventful and unrewarding, but the pope sent a message that, theologically speaking, he was the bishop of Rome, and he wanted to be a bishop in the real sense.[24] He enjoyed doing what a bishop did in a real local church: "Last night for the first time in nearly a century, the pope went for a walk through the streets of Rome: Seminar, Pantheon, and Piazza Capranica. General astonishment and delight. I wanted to make this gesture in the act of homage to the Collegio Capranica and my benefactor, Monsignor Giovanni Morlani, who was a student there."[25]

The preparation of Vatican II between the spring of 1960 and the summer of 1962 was carried out under a pope who wanted to be the bishop of Rome, but also of a church that was becoming more ecumenical and more global. In the

---

nese" theologian and priest Giuseppe Dossetti in a lecture given in February 1965.

24. See Michele Manzo, *Papa Giovanni vescovo di Roma. Sinodo e pastorale diocesana nell'episcopato romano di Roncalli* (Cinisello Balsamo: San Paolo, 1991).

25. *Diaries Pontificate 1958–1963*, 87 (January 29, 1960).

early 1960s Rome was one of the centers of the world, and the pope had a clear sense of that. Immediately after World War II, Rome was one of the capitals for the creation of a peaceful Europe; the Treaty of Rome in 1957 laid the foundations of the future European Union. In the summer of 1960 Rome hosted the Olympics and John XXIII saw it firsthand: "In the afternoon in St. Peter's Square there was a reception of the athletes for the Olympic games, a spectacle never seen before in the history of Rome. . . . I did not want to be carried on the *sedia gestatoria*. This allowed me to put my trust in these bold youth coming from around the world and let me be greeted by all (belonging to all religions) with respect and with an abandon that everyone will remember until the end of their lives."[26]

There was genuine theological growth in the global consciousness of the Catholic Church during the pontificate of John XXIII. In March 1960 he asked Cardinal Bea, a German Jesuit biblical scholar (for nineteen years rector of the Pontifical Biblical Institute in Rome and created cardinal by him in 1959) to lead the new "Secretariat for Christian Unity" in charge of rebuilding theological bridges with non-Catholic Christians. This Secretariat had no parallels or counterparts in the Roman Curia, which was up to that point dominating the preparation of Vatican II. This decision was the most important and creative decision of John XXIII for the whole development of Vatican II. Not less important was John XXIII's decision to receive on June 13, 1960, the Jewish French historian Jules Isaac (survivor of the Holocaust and author of works accusing the Catholic theological tradition of being co-responsible for anti-Semitism) who asked the pope whether or not Jews could have some hope from

26. Ibid., 154 (August 24, 1960).

the council. John XXIII reassured him that the council would
not be indifferent to the implications of the Holocaust for
Catholic theology.[27] On December 2, 1960, John XXIII received the visit of the Anglican Primate, Geoffrey Fischer.
John XXIII was open to the world of other Christians and
other religions as no pope before him, and much more than
the average Catholic faithful at the end of the 1950s.

Within Catholicism the church needed to become more
aware of its global dimension as well. Under John XXIII
bishops were appointed for Africa and Asia who were native
to those areas and the Catholic Churches in non-European
countries became more responsible and active in incarnating
their Catholic identity in a local culture. In May 1960 when
he appointed bishops for Africa and Asia he wrote, "Heroic
and blessed day today for the pope: *Servus Servorum et Princeps Sacerdotii*. The consecration of fourteen new bishops
included ten from Africa and all were involved in missions
in Africa and Asia. General commotion for the event in
St. Peter's was among the most rare of all time."[28] The global
dimension of the church was expressed in the preparation of
the council, which began with an open consultation of all the
Catholic bishops. Their replies (in Latin, *vota*) to the request
of the pope to speak their minds about the agenda of the
upcoming council was the real basis for the beginning of what
John XXIII envisioned.

In 1959 John XXIII published three encyclicals (*Sacerdotii Nostri Primordia* on priesthood, *Grata Recordatio* on
the rosary, and *Princeps Pastorum* on the missions), but the
years 1959–1961 were crucial years for the globalization
of the Catholic Church and the institution of national

27. Ibid., 127 (June 23, 1960).
28. Ibid., 117 (May 8, 1960).

episcopates of native bishops in recently decolonized countries (Congo, Burundi, Vietnam, Korea, and Indonesia). But
globalization was also needed for the Catholic Church in
the "old world." John XXIII was aware of the difficult relationship between the Latin identity of the Roman Catholic
Church and the traditions of the Catholic Churches of the
East. His awareness was historical (as a historian), theological and pastoral (as a bishop), but also experiential (having lived in the East for almost twenty years). In April 1961
he showed this awareness in a liturgical setting: "Today
episcopal consecration of Bishop Coussa in the Sistine Chapel. One of the brightest and dearest days of my life. . . .
Forcing myself to undertake the challenge of the Greek language and ritual did cost some effort, but everything was
resolved with satisfaction and edification. Msgr. Coussa told
me on the eve: 'Your liturgical gesture, Holy Father, is worth
more than two papal encyclicals, for the affirmation of clear
and well-received brotherhood of the Catholic churches.' I
think he is right."[29]

The impact of John XXIII on the world continued in May
1961 when he published his first great encyclical, *Mater et
Magistra*, an encyclical focusing on social issues in line with
Leo XIII's *Rerum Novarum* (1891), but with a more concrete approach to the modern development of socialization.
This encyclical was one of the most telling moments in Roncalli's pontificate, not only in terms of the content of the
encyclical, but also in terms of his style of being pope:

> The encyclical *Mater et Magistra* is awakening in the whole
> world acclaim and enthusiasm, not only among Catholics,
> but also in personalities of great significance. I especially

29. Ibid., 240 (April 16, 1961).

bless the Lord for the prominence given in the encyclical
to the spirit and forms of respect and moderation with
which the document is about people, ideas, and situations.
The humble pope who should be master of truth is also an
example of discretion, of grace, and of charity *ad omnes.*
Is he not the *Vicarius Christi?*[30]

John XXIII saw *Mater et Magistra* as one of his signature
acts: "Last night and tonight I reread with lively attention
the encyclical *Mater et Magistra* and am grateful to the
Lord for having prepared and published it. *Scio vere* [I
truly know] that this was a great gesture of my humble
pontificate."[31]

John XXIII knew that he had to update the church, but
he was aware of the gifts of the Catholic Church in its
structure and experience, which also applied to the Roman
Curia. During his career Roncalli had a difficult relationship
with Curia officials, but knew that the Catholic Church
needed a look on universal issues from a Roman window:
"Today at the Secretariat of State. Another field day: among
the most satisfying in my good job as a pope. I therefore
visited all of this true '*Noah's ark*,' not for its antiquity
(because in fact it has a very modern structure) but for the
synthetic complexity of the whole government of the holy
Church extended to the whole world."[32]

At the same time Roncalli proceeded to dramatically
change some of the imperial features of the Roman papacy,
which was evident on the occasion of the celebration of his
eightieth birthday. Everybody could see that his becoming
bishop, cardinal, and then pope had not changed the humble

30. Ibid., 251 (July 20, 1961).
31. Ibid., 259 (September 3, 1961).
32. Ibid., 211 (January 13, 1961).

social status of his family members: "In St. Peter's for the celebration of the three years of the pontificate and eighty years of the pope, with fifty cardinals and seventy official representatives of various old and new states of the world. From my throne I saw the faces of my siblings, Severo, Alfredo, Giuseppe, and Assunta with grandchildren. They were on the same line of the representatives of the Italian Government."[33] In his letter to his family, on December 3, 1961, Roncalli told his brothers and sisters that "one of the finest and most admired merits of Pope John and his Roncallis" will be that when one of the Roncallis became pope, he did not change the social status of his family members, he did not make them rich. He remained always "the son of humble but respected parents. . . . At my death I shall not lack the praise that did so much honor to the saintly Pius X: 'He was born poor and died poor.' "[34] But John XXIII's humility did not mean a belittled notion of his duties as a pope. During the winter 1961–1962 John XXIII rejected the proposal for an apostolic constitution on mercy called *De Paulo Apostolo* because the language of mercy in that draft did not reflect his idea of the centrality of mercy in the Catholic Church.[35] Roncalli knew the limits of the supposedly "absolute" papal power, but he also wanted to be the leader of a church in changing times.

This new understanding of the papal office by John XXIII was matched by the extraordinary challenges coming from

33. Ibid., 275 (November 4, 1961).

34. *Giovanni XXIII, Il giornale dell'anima e altri scritti di pietà* (Rome: Edizioni di Storia e Letteratura, 1964), 343. (English translation in *Pope John XXIII, Letters to His Family*, trans. Dorothy White (New York/Toronto: McGraw-Hill, 1970), 829.

35. Melloni, *Papa Giovanni*, 254.

the Cold War. For Roncalli the papal office was a pastoral ministry that was not eager to relinquish the high duties coming from the diplomatic tradition of the Holy See, but on the contrary was aware of the need to use the diplomatic tools of the Holy See to serve the cause of peace. The early 1960s witnessed the peak of the nuclear confrontation between the United States of America and Soviet Russia. Pope John, the former Vatican diplomat, knew that world leaders could use a line of communication to triangulate their negotiations and ease the growing tensions. From September 1961 until the end of his life, John XXIII accepted the fact that pursuing world peace was an integral part of his duties. Just a few weeks after the building of the Berlin Wall he wrote:

> In the evening on TV there is the communication of Khrushchev, the despot of Russia, speaking to my appeal to the leaders of states for peace: respectful, calm, understandable. I think it is the first time that the words of the pope inviting peace have been treated with respect. As to the sincerity of the intentions of those who hold to professed atheism and materialism, even when he [Khrushchev] says well the word of the pope, believe me is another thing completely. Meanwhile, this is better than silence or contempt.[36]

On November 21, 1961, Khrushchev sent a personal message to the pope for his birthday. It was the beginning of a twelve-month period that culminated during the first weeks of Vatican II and at the time of the Cuban Missile Crisis (October 14–28, 1962). The radio message of September 11, 1962, sent to all the faithful in preparation for the council, had an important part about peace: the aim of the council

---

36. *Diaries Pontificate 1958–1963*, 263 (September 20, 1961).

is "to cooperate in the triumph of peace, thus to make earthly existence more noble, more just, and more deserving for all."[37] During the fourteen days of the missile crisis, John XXIII was personally engaged in offering the two parties a channel of communication in order to avoid the nuclear holocaust. On October 25, 1962, John XXIII read (in French) his appeal for peace from Vatican Radio: "We beg all governments not to remain deaf to this cry of humanity. That they do all that is in their power to save peace. . . Promoting, favoring, accepting conversations, at all levels and in any time, is a rule of wisdom and prudence that attracts the blessings of heaven and earth."[38] The next day the text of the papal speech was printed on the front page of the official newspaper *Pravda*, the central organ of the Communist Party of the Soviet Union. The international activism of the Vatican for peace and the ecumenical council were distinct but not separated. Just a few days before the opening of Vatican II, the Orthodox Patriarchate of Moscow accepted the invitation from the Vatican for "ecumenical observers" at the council: for the first time in the history of the councils of the Catholic Church, there were non-Catholic theologians and church leaders attending and observing the debates.

The end of the missile crisis was also the beginning of the idea and drafting of the last encyclical of Pope John, *Pacem in Terris*, that was published in April 1963 a few weeks before his death. It was one of the most consequential papal documents for the development of Vatican II and for the

37. See *History of Vatican II*, vol. 2, 435–41, quote 439. On June 3, 1962, Roncalli had published an appeal for peace in Algeria.

38. Original text (in French) in *Acta Apostolicae Sedis* 15 (December 28, 1962): 861–62. See also *Diaries Pontificate 1958–1963*, 447 (October 25, 1962).

aggiornamento of the Catholic Church in the modern world. Some saw in John XXIII's relationship to world politics only a "widening of the Tiber"—more distance from Italian politics. But the theological consequences of Roncalli's worldview went well beyond the boundaries between Italy and the Vatican.

Vatican II: "Mother Church Rejoices"

In the words of John XXIII, 1962 was "the year of Vatican II."[39] As the preparation proceeded toward the opening on October 11, 1962, the pope was aware of his responsibilities during the last few weeks before the opening of the council: "We will do together a review of their [the conciliar commissions] work that responds to my precise duties as *influential and supreme leader* of the Ecumenical Council."[40] This preparation for Vatican II was also a personal spiritual preparation for the pope, which led to some surprises. His idea to visit the sanctuaries of Loreto and Assisi before the beginning of the council came to him just a few days before it began: "With Monsignor Dell'Acqua I confided a bygone thought that now I had forgotten . . . *a personal visit of the pope to Loreto* before the eve of the council."[41] That trip to Loreto and Assisi by John XXIII was the first official papal trip outside Rome since the end of the Papal State in 1870; it marked a symbolic end of the Vatican's isolation from Italy and the world. It also marked the spiritual beginning of Vatican II for John XXIII: "This date is to be written with golden color in my life: the pilgrimage that I wanted to do,

39. *Diaries Pontificate 1958–1963*, 325 (January 1, 1962).
40. Ibid., 407 (July 17, 1962).
41. Ibid., 437 (September 28, 1962).

a few days sufficed to conceive, to do it, and to succeed with the help of the Lord—the visit to Our Lady of Loreto and St. Francis of Assisi as a plea of grace for the ecumenical council Vatican II. I thought of that, as usual, with simplicity, and I decided to do it."[42] With the pilgrimage, John XXIII put Vatican II under the protection of the Madonna of Loreto and of St. Francis of Assisi.

John XXIII was a church historian aware that he was making history. The pope who was elected as a transitional figure knew that Vatican II would be the major accomplishment of his pontificate and a historical moment in the church: "This day [October 11, 1962] marks the solemn opening of the ecumenical council. . . . I thank the Lord who made me not unworthy of the honor of opening this council in his name, the beginning of many graces to his Holy Church. He ordered that the first spark that prepared the council for three years came out of my mouth and my heart. I was even prepared to give up the joy of this beginning. And I repeat with the same calm: *fiat voluntas tua.*"[43]

The opening of Vatican II unfolded under the inspiration of the pope who called it. Vatican II was a fundamental moment for a church that met for the first time in its universal dimension: east and west, north and south, rich and poor, old and young. The opening speech of the council, *Gaudet Mater Ecclesia*, "Mother Church Rejoices," was one of the most consequential speeches in church history. Written in its entirety by the pope himself (beginning in February, eight months before being delivered),[44] *Gaudet* changed the horizon of expectations from the council in many members, theolo-

42. Ibid., 439 (October 4, 1962).
43. Ibid., 441 (October 11, 1962).
44. Melloni, *Papa Giovanni. Un cristiano e il suo concilio*, 258–88.

gians, and observers of Vatican II. The speech outlined the task of ecumenical councils in the church, the reason for Vatican II, the task of the council in the promotion of doctrine, and the "promotion of unity in the Christian and human family": "Nowadays however, the Spouse of Christ prefers to make use of *the medicine of mercy* rather than that of severity. She considers that she meets the needs of the present day by demonstrating the validity of her teaching rather than by condemnations." In the central part of the speech came the harshest lines of a pope against the ideologues of past Catholicism, many of them working in the Roman Curia:

> It often happens, as we have learned in the daily exercise of the apostolic ministry, that, not without offense to our ears, the voices of people are brought to us who, although burning with religious fervor, nevertheless do not think things through with enough discretion and prudence and judgment. These people see only ruin and calamity in the present conditions of human society. They keep repeating that our times, if compared to past centuries, have been getting worse. And they act as if they have nothing to learn from history, which is the teacher of life, and as if at the time of past councils everything went favorably and correctly with respect to Christian doctrine, morality, and the church's proper freedom. *We believe that we must quite disagree with these prophets of doom who are always forecasting disaster, as if the end of the world were at hand.*[45]

In this speech John XXIII upset the current mentality of official Catholic culture, which was focused on the condemnation of the "enemies." "Roncalli depicted a church that

---

45. For the context of the speech at the council, see *History of Vatican II*, vol. 2, 14–21. Emphasis mine.

believes its task is exhausted by the act of condemning things that have been condemned many times already. . . . John XXIII believed that the 'golden age' of medievalism, a dream protracted by Christendom but decayed into modernity, really never existed."[46] Vatican II must go beyond these dreams of *translatio* of Catholicism back into medieval times and look for the "signs of our times" and interpret them in light of the Gospel. The speech did not give Vatican II an agenda, but a perspective; theologically it entailed a move from the obsession with given historical and cultural patterns toward the kingdom of God.[47]

The opening day of Vatican II concluded with another speech, one of the most famous speeches of John XXIII, the "Moonlight Address." It was totally unexpected and impromptu, given by John XXIII from his window in St. Peter's Square. This speech did not formally belong to the corpus of the documents of Vatican II, but it is a fundamental interpretive key to understand Roncalli's relationship with Vatican II:

> Dear sons and daughters, I feel your voices! Mine is just one lone voice, but it sums up the voice of the whole world. And in fact, all the world is represented here tonight. It could be said that even the moon hastens close tonight, that from above it might watch this spectacle that not even St. Peter's Basilica, over its four centuries of history, has ever been able to witness. We are concluding a great day of peace. Yes, of peace! 'Glory to God and peace to men of goodwill.' If I asked you, if I could ask of each one of you: where are you from? The children of Rome, especially

46. Melloni, *Papa Giovanni. Un cristiano e il suo concilio*, 263.
47. For a global interpretation of *Gaudet Mater Ecclesia*, see Alberigo, *Dalla laguna al Tevere*, 157–90.

represented here, would respond: ah, we are the closest of children, and you are our bishop. Well, then, sons and daughters of Rome, always remember that you represent 'Roma, caput mundi' [Rome, the capital of the world] that through the design of Providence it has been called to be across the centuries. My own person counts for nothing—it is a brother who speaks to you, became a father by the will of our Lord, but all together, fatherhood and brotherhood and God's grace, give honor to the impressions of this night, which are always our feelings, which now we express before heaven and earth: faith, hope, love, love of God, love of brother, all aided along the way in the Lord's holy peace for the work of the good.[48]

The council debate opened a few days later. It was a council only partially shaped by the decisions of John XXIII. Vatican II interpreted a movement already going on in the church, but one that was constrained by the organizational control of the Roman Curia on the conciliar "machine." The first debate at Vatican II was on the liturgical reform and John XXIII was aware of the crucial nature of the issue. His experience as an Italian cleric abroad was not typical of many Italian and European bishops: "The question of the Latin language certainly divides the ones who have never left home, or Italy, from the members of other nations, especially in missionary areas, or those who despite being Italian live and sacrifice in distant regions. On this point of Latin in the liturgy it will be necessary to proceed slowly

---

48. Historians had access to the complete text of the speech only recently thanks to the newly discovered video recording. Melloni, *Papa Giovanni. Un cristiano e il suo concilio*, 271–72; Federico Ruozzi, *Il concilio in diretta. Il Vaticano II e la televisione tra informazione e partecipazione* (Bologna: il Mulino, 2012).

and by degrees."[49] The pope who called Vatican II knew that some of the reforms of Vatican II would require much work and that the work of *aggiornamento* would not be done in one or two sessions: "The length of the discourses of the council fathers leaves me a little uncertain about the rapidity of work, uncertain and perplexed. . . . If we go on like this, not even all of 1963 will be enough. Beware of the temptation of impatience!"[50]

John XXIII was able to interpret the council, its mood, and its needs. In a crucial moment during the first period, on November 21, 1962, John XXIII interpreted the rules of Vatican II in a way that made it possible for the council to restart the debate on the sources of the revelation and Scripture at Vatican II, the schema *De fontibus revelationis*, something that would have been impossible had the pope interpreted the rules in a formalist and literalist way.[51] On December 8, 1962, at the end of the first session of Vatican II, he gave another speech regarding the council, in which he explained the reasons for the fortunate choice of opening Vatican II with the debate on the liturgy.[52]

Death of a Bishop among His People

The first intersession, between the first and the second sessions of Vatican II, encompassed the last semester in the life of Angelo Giuseppe Roncalli. It was a fundamental

49. *Diaries Pontificate 1958–1963*, 446 (October 24, 1962).

50. Ibid., 452 (November 5, 1962).

51. Ibid., 454 (November 14, 1962); *History of Vatican II*, vol. 2, 233–66.

52. *History of Vatican II*, vol. 2, 357; Melloni, *Papa Giovanni. Un cristiano e il suo concilio*, 281–83.

moment in the history of the council: "the second preparation of Vatican II" gave shape to the council emancipated
from the legacy of the Roman Curia-controlled preparation
of 1960–1962.[53] But it also was the culmination of John
XXIII's pontificate for other reasons. Roncalli made a
breakthrough in the public theology of the Catholic Church,
especially regarding the relationship between Catholicism,
democracy, human rights, and peace. On January 4, 1963,
the cover of *Time* magazine named John XXIII "Man of
the Year 1962" and called him "an intuitive judge of man-
kind's hopes and needs."[54] On March 5, 1963, John XXIII
received in audience the daughter of Nikita Khrushchev
and her husband, the journalist Alexandr Adjubei; they
were the first Soviet citizens admitted in the Vatican since
the Russian revolution of 1917. John XXIII's audience with
them was met with resistance by Cardinal Ottaviani of the
Holy Office, a deafening silence from the Jesuit-run (and
unofficial Vatican voice) "Civiltà Cattolica," and the refusal
of the Secretariat of State to publish a press release about
the audience.[55] This unprecedented move for a pope in the
midst of the Cold War was one of the public statements of

53. *History of Vatican II*, vol. 2, 359–514.
54. The lead article of that issue of *Time* opened this way: "The
Year of Our Lord 1962 was a year of American resolve, Russian
orbiting, European union and Chinese war. In a tense yet hope-filled
time, these were the events that dominated conversation and invited
history's scrutiny. But history has a long eye, and it is quite possible
that in her vision 1962's most fateful rendezvous took place in the
world's most famous church—having lived for years in men's hearts
and minds. That event was the beginning of a revolution in Christianity, the ancient faith whose 900 million adherents make it the world's
largest religion. It began on Oct. 11, 1962."
55. Alberigo, *Dalla laguna al Tevere*, 103–4.

Roncalli about the engagement of the church in the *Ost-politik* that would ultimately lead the church to the summit of Helsinki of July–August 1975, where the Soviet Union would sign the treaty on human rights, partly due to the diplomatic leverage of the Vatican.

On April 9, 1963, in front of the cameras on Italian public television, John XXIII signed *Pacem in Terris*, his last encyclical, "peak and summit" of Roncalli's teaching.[56] Aware of the objections against the "optimism" of his teaching, the pope had said in a press conference the week before: "some say that the pope is too optimistic . . . but I cannot be different from our Lord who spread around him goodness, joy, peace, and encouragement."[57]

On May 10 and 11 he visited the President of the Italian Republic in the Palace of Quirinale that had belonged to the pope until 1870. John XXIII was the first pope to acknowledge symbolically the legitimacy of the Italian Republic and was awarded the "Balzan International Award for Peace" (an unlikely award for the pope to receive and accept). These last public events were influenced by *Pacem in Terris*, both in the public reception of the papal teaching on peace and in the ecclesiastical reluctance to express consensus for a teaching rife with political and ideological implications, especially in Europe and North America. The silence of cardinals and bishops about *Pacem in Terris*, and the implied lack of support for the last encyclical of John XXIII was just the last indication of the "institutional loneliness" of Angelo Giuseppe Roncalli in the Vatican.

56. Alberto Melloni, *Pacem in terris. Storia dell'ultima enciclica di papa Giovanni* (Roma/Bari: Laterza, 2010), 4.

57. Ibid., 82.

May 20, 1963, was the last entry of his diary: "This morning, for the third time I received Communion in bed, instead of enjoying the celebration of the Holy Mass. Patience, patience. But I had to accept the farewell visit of Cardinal Wyszynski, Primate of Poland, with four bishops. . . . I spent the rest of the day in bed with several episodes of acute physical pain. The ones who assist me, always with great charity, are my family, Cardinal Cicognani, Msgr. Capovilla, brother Federico Belotti, and domestics."[58] On May 22 the Vatican announced the suspension of the general audiences, given the rapid decline of the pope's health. On May 31 the agony began and on June 3, 1963, the Monday of Pentecost, a few minutes before 8:00 p.m., Angelo Giuseppe Roncalli died.

It was a death lived in public, with discretion and devotion both by him and his church, even though it was the first live television broadcast of the death of a pope.[59] Pope John had visited the parishes of Rome, including the dodgy *borgate* in the outskirts of Rome, as part of his ministry of bishop of the local church of Rome. In the same spirit, Piazza San Pietro was filled with people praying during the agony of the bishop of Rome. Roncalli died as a bishop, according to the *Ceremoniale Episcoporum*, surrounded by his people—and by the Jews of the community of Rome, who decided to go to Piazza San Pietro to pray the Psalms for the dying pope.[60]

58. *Diaries Pontificate 1958–1963*, 520–21 (May 20, 1963).

59. Federico Ruozzi, "L'icona Giovanni XXIII," in *L'ora che sta il mondo attraversando. Giovanni XXIII di fronte alla storia*, eds. Giovanni Grado Merlo and Francesco Mores (Rome: Edizioni di Storia e Letteratura, 2009), 47–102.

60. Enrico Galavotti, "Un bergamasco papa e santo," in *L'ora che sta il mondo attraversando* (Rome: Edizioni di Storia e Letteratura, 2009), 302.

CONCLUSION

John XXIII: Medicine of Mercy and Signs of the Times

Since the days right after his death, John XXIII left an indelible mark on the church—within the ecumenical council called by him (where many bishops wanted to proclaim him saint the ancient way, that is, canonized by the bishops gathered in council); in the church (where many Catholics have always considered him a saint); and around the world (where Pope John was seen as the first modern, global pope of the Catholic Church). Dismissively labeled by some as simple and naïve, the vast majority of Catholics and non-Catholics knew then and have been aware since then, that something happened in the church—it happened with, thanks to, and through Angelo Giuseppe Roncalli.[1]

---

1. For the first important articulation of the meaning of Roncalli for church history, see Giacomo Lercaro (cardinal archbishop of Bologna, 1952–1968), *John XXIII: Simpleton or Saint?* trans. Dorothy White (Chicago: Franciscan Herald Press, 1967). Original Italian: *Giovanni XXIII: Linee per una ricerca storica* (Rome: Edizioni di Storia e Letteratura, 1965). The lecture, given in Rome on February 23, 1965, had been drafted by the Italian priest and conciliar *peritus* Giuseppe Dossetti.

The life of John XXIII was at the same time ordinary and extraordinary, normal and exceptional. Ordinary and normal because for his whole life Roncalli wanted to be a Christian rooted in the Catholic tradition, in the middle of different tendencies during a time of great change, from the antimodernist purge of the early 1900s to the cultural revolution of the post-World War II period. Roncalli was an intellectual, specifically a historian, but always skeptical of intellectualism in Catholic theology; he was a man of prayer, devotion, and ascetic practices typical of a Catholic born in 1881, but diffident, both when a young priest and when the pope, of spiritual athleticism in search of wondrous and supernatural ways to reach God.[2] Until recently, the process of canonization looked for "heroic virtues of holiness" in the candidates, but in recent times the value of the personal testimony has been emphasized. Roncalli/John XXIII in his "normality" is truly a modern saint, "not an icon of the Roman papacy; John XXIII is acknowledged as teacher for our interior life."[3] For Roncalli humility was not demureness, but the ability to reorient the dynamism of interior life away from one's ego in order to avoid the temptations of subjectivism and to reach real freedom.

Roncalli's life was exceptional in the way he lived it—understanding the profound need to rediscover the mercy of God revealed through Jesus Christ for the church and for humankind. In a time of a globalization of the world matched

---

2. Notable was the deep mistrust of Roncalli for Padre Pio of Pietrelcina (canonized in 2002 by John Paul II). See Sergio Luzzatto, *Padre Pio. Miracles and Politics in a Secular Age*, trans. Frederika Randall (New York: Henry Holt and Co., 2010).

3. Alberto Melloni, *Il Giornale dell'anima di Giovanni XXIII* (Milan: Jaca Book, 2000), 11.

only by growing social inequalities and cultural-ideological divisions of the world wars and the Cold War, Roncalli, first as a cleric and then as a pope, captured the deep need for the medicine of mercy, without ever thinking that the real Christian character of Catholicism could be at risk because of the use of the medicine of mercy. The pastoral imperative of the Catholic ministry was a recurring theme with Roncalli since the very beginning of his career, and it became more visible as his responsibilities and experiences grew. The so-called "*mystère Roncalli*" is explained by the fact that Roncalli grew into the papacy as John XXIII thanks to his previous experiences, but not bound by them.

Roncalli was not an Augustinian theologian imbued with pessimism nor was he a Thomist (or neo-Thomist) thinker trying to create a new paradigm. He was deeply absorbed in the sources of the Christian tradition (Scripture, the Fathers, the liturgy) and was fully part of the twentieth century of the world wars, of the ethno-religious hatred, and of the dehumanizing ideologies of which Catholics had been often willing participants and not just victims. He believed that fidelity to the great tradition was the way to rediscover the real essence of the Gospel of Jesus Christ by liberating it from much historical, ideological, and political encrustations. That is a message also for the temptation to "culturalize" Catholicism, that is, to make of the Gospel a culture with all the risks coming from that option for a church that is now in a multicultural world, multicultural even in its local dimensions.

Roncalli was the pope who exhibited "openness to humankind as the key of universalism claimed by the papal ministry."[4] In the middle of his pontificate, in 1961, Roncalli

----

4. Alberto Melloni, *Papa Giovanni. Un cristiano e il suo concilio* (Turin: Einaudi, 2009), 27.

expressed his view of his ministry in the church in a very simple way: "The sublime, divine, and holy task of the pope to the whole church and the bishops is to preach the Gospel, to lead men to eternal salvation. . . . The example of the pope must be one of teaching and encouragement to all. . . . Always, but especially in these times, the bishop must spread a balsamic oil of sweetness over the wounds of humanity."[5] These words have become familiar in the Catholic Church after his death. In this sense there is a pre-John XXIII and a post-John XXIII Catholic Church, a periodization that is part of the role of Vatican II, but not totally overlapping with the more classical periodization "pre-Vatican II" and "post-Vatican II" church.

After Roncalli, the word *aggiornamento* has become the key word to understand the kind of change the Catholic Church went through thanks to his role at Vatican II. The interpretation of Vatican II requires a complex approach, but for Roncalli the "updating" of Christian life and of the church was inspired by a fairly simple idea, one going back to the sources of Christianity: the Scripture and the sacraments, a simple (but not simplistic) piety trying to learn from great examples of the Christian tradition. In this sense, Saint John XXIII is a model of Christian life, a normal Christian staying faithful to the ordinary means of salvation through times changing at an extraordinarily fast pace. Roncalli has not become the icon of competing ecclesiastical ideologies (liberal versus conservative) because his fidelity to the great tradition of the church made him exactly the opposite of a traditionalist. Roncalli, the scholar of the Council of Trent, called Vatican II in order to let Vatican II do for the church in global modernity what Trent in the

5. Roncalli, *Il Giornale dell'Anima*, 466–67 (August 10, 1961).

sixteenth century did for the church in early modern times after the breakup of the unity of western Christianity and the age of "confessionalization." As a bishop and later as pope, Roncalli made use of all the tools provided by the Council of Trent, but adding to them a deep and prophetic grasp of the "signs of the times" and the "medicine of mercy" that shaped all his being.

John XXIII is the key to understanding the church of today, especially the church after the election of Pope Francis in 2013, the first pope coming from a non-European and non-Mediterranean area of the world. Both John XXIII and Francis were born of poor families, went through problematic and unseemly ecclesiastical careers, elected to the papacy at the very end of their careers (almost "in overtime"), and lived in similar situations in the life of the church and in its relationship with the world *ad extra*. Both Roncalli and Bergoglio brought with them to the Vatican an idea of the church that is more global and more historical than it was before their times. The emphasis on the "poor church, church for the poor" expressed by Pope Francis a few hours after his election comes from Vatican II and from its pope, John XXIII, who in his life always cherished (without ever romanticizing it) the humble social conditions of his family as an integral part of his spiritual life and as a gift. The extraordinary character of Roncalli/John XXIII shows through the fact that he opened the process for the redefinition of the papacy not through a plan or a project, but thanks to the "confluence in him of papal office, personal sanctity, and prophesy—a confluence that is exceptional in church history."[6]

6. Giuseppe Alberigo, *Papa Giovanni XXIII 1881–1963* (Bologna: EDB, 2000), 9.

In order to understand Roncalli, another comparison may be useful. In the iconography (a very ecumenical one: Catholic, non-Catholic, and secular) of the twentieth century, John XXIII has been often associated with John Fitzgerald Kennedy—two transformational Catholic figures of the 1960s who provided new leadership. But in a way the case of Roncalli was exactly the opposite of the "elusive president."[7] The "Kennedy mystique" had a lot to do with the elusiveness of the first Catholic president of the United States. On the contrary, we know a lot about Roncalli, who was not elusive at all. We know much more about Roncalli/John XXIII than of any other pope, thanks to the paper trail he left behind: letters, spiritual journals, his scholarly activity, and day-by-day diaries for his whole life. John Kennedy's was an "unfinished life."[8] Roncalli lived a full life, accomplished in every sense—survived World War I; acted as a diplomat in World War II; lived his career despite, and after, a long ecclesiastic "exile," first in eastern Europe and then in France; and had poor or bad relations with the Roman Curia. President Kennedy's death was and still is for many a mystery. Roncalli's death is a mystery only in the sacramental sense of the word. The holy and public death of Roncalli on June 3, 1963, was the true fulfillment of his life, both from the point of view of his Christian spirituality and for the impact that his agony and his death had on the emerging global community. Roncalli's life was an accomplishment, represented in a special way by his death on the stage of the sacred that is the Rome of the Catholic Church.

7. See Jill Abramson, "The Elusive President," *New York Times Book Review* (October 27, 2013).
8. See Robert Dallek, *An Unfinished Life: John F. Kennedy, 1917–1963* (Boston: Little, Brown, and Co., 2003).

The tangible and undeniable change brought about by Roncalli/John XXIII made him the first global pope in church history. It is an extraordinary biography for a Catholic bishop who became pope. His walk of life makes of him an exemplar of the rise of a new global consciousness in the world. Roncalli interpreted this new consciousness for the Catholic Church that had gone through the two world wars, the Shoah, and the new cultural changes of the postwar period. After World War II some thought—and perhaps still think—that the church could go on pretending that not much had happened, and that what happened has little to say to the church and to Catholic theology. A pope who had spent almost thirty years of his life out of his country, speaking and preaching in languages different from his native one and dealing with people of cultural and religious traditions different from his own, knew that to some extent change in the world and in the church had *already* happened. It was time for the church to gather and give theological expression to those changes: "It is not that the Gospel has changed; it is that we have begun to understand it better. Those who, like me, spent twenty years in the East, eight in France, and were able to compare different cultures and traditions, know that the moment has come to discern the signs of the times, to seize the opportunity, and to look far ahead."[9]

9. Roncalli, *Il Giornale dell'Anima*, 500 (May 24, 1963).

Selected Bibliography

Primary Sources

Capovilla, Loris Francesco, Giuseppe De Luca, Angelo Giuseppe Roncalli. *Carteggio, 1933–1962*. Edited by Marco Roncalli. Rome: Edizioni di Storia e Letteratura, 2006.

Giovanni XXIII. *Discorsi, messaggi, colloqui del Santo Padre Giovanni XXIII. 28 ottobre 1958–3 giugno 1963*. 5 vols. Vatican City: Tipografia poliglotta vaticana, 1961–67.

———. *Il giornale dell'anima e altri scritti di pietà*. Rome: Edizioni di Storia e Letteratura, 1964 [Angelo Giuseppe Roncalli/John XXIII, *The Journal of a Soul*]. Translated by Dorothy White. New York: McGraw-Hill, 1965.

———. *Lettere del pontificato*. Edited by Loris Francesco Capovilla. Cinisello Balsamo (Milan): San Paolo, 2008.

———. *Lettere, 1958–1963*. Edited by Loris Francesco Capovilla. Rome: Edizioni di Storia e Letteratura, 1978.

———. *Questa Chiesa che tanto amo: lettere ai vescovi di Bergamo*. Edited by Antonio Pesenti. Cinisello Balsamo (Milan): San Paolo, 2002.

Roncalli, Angelo Giuseppe. *Chierico e storico a Bergamo. Antologia di scritti (1907–1912)*. Edited by Francesco Mores. Rome: Edizioni di Storia e Letteratura, 2008.

———. *Edizione nazionale dei diari di Angelo Giuseppe Roncalli–Giovanni XXIII* [Edition of the complete diaries of Angelo Giuseppe Roncalli/John XXIII]:

Vol. 1, *Il Giornale dell'Anima: Soliloqui, note e diari spirituali.*
Edited by Alberto Melloni. Bologna: Istituto per le scienze
religiose, Fondazione per le scienze religiose Giovanni
XXIII, 2003. (First edition by Alberto Melloni: Bologna:
Istituto per le scienze religiose, 1987.)

Vol. 2, *Nelle mani di Dio a servizio dell'uomo: I diari di don
Roncalli, 1905–1925.* Edited by Lucia Butturini. Bologna:
Istituto per le scienze religiose, Fondazione per le scienze
religiose Giovanni XXIII, 2008.

Vol. 3, *Tener da conto: Agendine di Bulgaria, 1925–1934.* Edited
by Massimo Faggioli. Bologna: Istituto per le scienze religiose, Fondazione per le scienze religiose Giovanni XXIII,
2008.

Vol. 4.1, *La mia vita in Oriente: Agende del delegato apostolico,
1935–1939.* Edited by Valeria Martano. Bologna: Istituto
per le scienze religiose, Fondazione per le scienze religiose
Giovanni XXIII, 2006.

Vol. 4.2, *La mia vita in Oriente: Agende del delegato apostolico,
1940–1944.* Edited by Valeria Martano. Bologna: Istituto
per le scienze religiose, Fondazione per le scienze religiose
Giovanni XXIII, 2008.

Vol. 5.1, *Anni di Francia: Agende del nunzio, 1945–1948.* Edited
by Étienne Fouilloux. Bologna: Istituto per le scienze religiose, Fondazione per le scienze religiose Giovanni XXIII,
2004.

Vol. 5.2, *Anni di Francia: Agende del nunzio, 1949–1953.* Edited
by Étienne Fouilloux. Bologna: Istituto per le scienze religiose, Fondazione per le scienze religiose Giovanni XXIII,
2006.

Vol. 6.1, *Pace e Vangelo: Agende del patriarca, 1953–1955.* Edited
by Enrico Galavotti. Bologna: Istituto per le scienze religiose,
Fondazione per le scienze religiose Giovanni XXIII, 2008.

Vol. 6.2, *Pace e Vangelo: Agende del patriarca, 1956–1958.* Edited
by Enrico Galavotti. Bologna: Istituto per le scienze religiose,
Fondazione per le scienze religiose Giovanni XXIII, 2008.

Vol. 7, *Pater amabilis: Agende del pontefice, 1958–1963.* Edited by Mauro Velati. Bologna: Istituto per le scienze religiose, Fondazione per le scienze religiose Giovanni XXIII, 2007.

———. *Fiducia e obbedienza: lettere ai rettori del Seminario romano 1901–1959.* Edited by Carlo Badalà. Cinisello Balsamo (Milan): San Paolo, 1997.

———. *Gli atti della visita apostolica di S. Carlo Borromeo a Bergamo (1575).* Con la collaborazione di don Pietro Forno, 2 vols. in 5 tomes. Florence: Olschki, 1936–1958 [1959].

———. *Gli inizi del seminario di Bergamo e San Carlo Borromeo.* Bergamo: Società Editrice S. Alessandro, 1939.

———. *Il lupo, l'orso, l'agnello: epistolario bulgaro con don K. Raev e mons. D. Theelen.* Ed. Paolo Cortesi. Cinisello Balsamo (Milan): San Paolo, 2013.

———. *In memoria di Mons. Giacomo Maria Radini Tedeschi vescovo di Bergamo.* Bergamo: Ed. Sant'Alessandro, 1916; second edition, Rome: Edizioni di Storia e Letteratura, 1963 [Angelo Giuseppe Roncalli/John XXIII. *My Bishop. A Portrait of Msgr. Giacomo Maria Radini Tedeschi.* With a foreword by H.E. Cardinale, and an introduction by Loris Capovilla. Translated by Dorothy White. New York: McGraw-Hill, 1969].

———. *La predicazione a Istanbul. Omelie, discorsi e note pastorali (1935–1944).* Edited by Alberto Melloni. Florence: Olschki, 1993.

———. *Lettere ai familiari 1901–1962.* Rome: Edizioni di Storia e Letteratura, 1968 [Pope John XXIII, *Letters to His Family.* Translated by Dorothy White. New York/Toronto: McGraw-Hill, 1970].

Studies

Alberigo, Angelina e Giuseppe. *Giovanni XXIII. Profezia nella fedeltà.* Brescia: Queriniana, 1978.

Alberigo, Giuseppe. *Papa Giovanni 1881–1963*. Bologna: EDB,
    2000 (second edition Bologna: EDB, 2013).
––––––. *Dalla laguna al Tevere. Angelo Giuseppe Roncalli da San
    Marco a San Pietro*. Bologna: il Mulino, 2000.
Battelli, Giuseppe. *Un pastore tra fede e ideologia. Giacomo Maria
    Radini Tedeschi 1857–1914*, Genoa: Marietti, 1988.
Benigni, Mario. *Papa Giovanni XXIII chierico e sacerdote a Ber-
    gamo 1892–1921*. Milan: Glossa, 1998.
Cahill, Thomas. *Pope John XXIII*. New York: Viking, 2002 [Italian
    translation: *Giovanni XXIII*. Rome: Fazi, 2005].
*Un cristiano sul trono di Pietro. Studi storici su Papa Giovanni
    XXIII*. Edited by Fondazione per le scienze religiose di
    Bologna. Gorle: Servitium, 2003.
Della Salda, Francesca. *Obbedienza e pace. Il vescovo A. G. Ron-
    calli tra Sofia e Roma (1925–1934)*. Genoa: Marietti, 1989.
Feldmann, Christian. *Pope John XXIII: A Spiritual Biography*.
    New York: Crossroad, 2000.
Galavotti, Enrico, *Processo a papa Giovanni. La causa di canon-
    izzazione di A. G. Roncalli (1965–2000)*. Bologna: il Mu-
    lino, 2005.
Hebblethwaite, Peter, and Margaret Hebblethwaite. *John XXIII:
    Pope of the Century*. London: Continuum, 2000.
History of Vatican II. Vols. 1–5. Edited by Giuseppe Alberigo,
    English version edited by Joseph A. Komonchak. Mary-
    knoll, NY: Orbis, 1995–2006.
Kartaloff, Kiril Plamen. *La sollecitudine ecclesiale di monsignor
    Roncalli in Bulgaria (1925–1934)*. Città del Vaticano:
    Libreria Editrice Vaticana, 2014.
Lercaro, Giacomo. *Giovanni XXIII: linee per una ricerca storica*.
    Rome: Edizioni di Storia e Letteratura, 1965 [*John XXIII:
    Simpleton or Saint?* Translated by Dorothy White. Chi-
    cago: Franciscan Herald Press, 1967].
*L'ora che sta il mondo attraversando. Giovanni XXIII di fronte
    alla storia*. Eds. Giovanni Grado Merlo and Francesco
    Mores. Rome: Edizioni di Storia e Letteratura, 2009.

Melloni, Alberto. *Il Giornale dell'anima di Giovanni XXIII.* Milan: Jaca Book, 2000.

———. *Pacem in Terris. Storia dell'ultima enciclica di Papa Giovanni.* Rome-Bari: Laterza, 2010.

———. *Papa Giovanni. Un cristiano e il suo concilio.* Turin: Einaudi, 2009.

———. *Tra Istanbul, Atene e la guerra. A.G. Roncalli vicario e delegato apostolico 1935–1944,* Genoa 1993.

O'Malley, John W. *What Happened at Vatican II.* Cambridge, MA: Harvard University Press, 2008.

Papa Giovanni. Edited by Giuseppe Alberigo. Rome-Bari: Laterza, 1987.

Riccardi, Andrea. *Il potere del papa da Pio XII a Giovanni Paolo II.* Rome-Bari: Laterza, 1993.

Trinchese, Stefano. *Roncalli e le missioni. L'opera della propagazione della fede tra Francia e Vaticano negli anni '20.* Brescia: Morcelliana, 1989.

Zizola, Giancarlo. *The Utopia of Pope John XXIII.* Maryknoll, NY: Orbis Books, 1978 [original Italian: *L'utopia di papa Giovanni.* Assisi: Cittadella, 1973, 2000].

Index

aggiornamento, 5, 6, 22, 30,
112, 123, 128, 136
Americanism, 23
America. *See* United States of
America
anti-Semitism, 5, 69, 75–77,
116. *See also* racism
Arendt, Hannah, 9
Atatürk, Mustafa Kemal, 70,
72

Bellarmine, Robert, 17
Benedict XV (pope), 3n8, 40,
45, 46, 47
Benedict XVI (pope), 2, 3,
5n15, 7, 8
Bergoglio, Jorge Mario. *See*
Francis (pope)
Borromeo, Saint Charles, 12,
14, 31, 32, 34, 77, 103
Bible, 96, 98. *See also* Scripture

Catholic social teaching. *See*
social Catholicism
Cold War, 3n6, 90, 112, 121,
129–30, 135

communism, 3n6, 5–6, 76, 86,
92, 99, 101–2, 107, 122. *See
also* Marxism
Constantine Era, 37
Counter-Reformation, 12, 15,
17, 30–32, 59, 72, 78, 85, 89,
98, 102–3, 136–37
Cuban Missile Crisis, 121–22

democracy, 13, 56, 81, 82, 92,
99, 100–101, 129

Eastern Rite, 54, 55, 57, 63, 68,
71–72, 77, 96, 118. *See also*
Orthodox Churches
ecumenism, 35, 54–55, 59, 71–
74, 78, 93, 95–96, 110–18,
122, 124–25, 133, 135–36,
137–39

family. *See* Roncalli family
fascism, 45–46, 47, 59, 79, 102
fathers of the church. *See*
patristics
Francis de Sales, Saint, 15, 19,
22

Francis of Assisi, Saint, 7n18, 17
Francis (pope), 1, 3, 7, 8, 137

Gonzaga, Saint Aloysius, 16, 19, 102

history, 23, 32–33, 37, 43, 59, 77–78, 89, 124, 125–26, 133n1, 137
Holocaust. *See* Shoah

inculturation, 73, 87, 139
Islam, 33–34, 42, 70, 72
Italy, 12–13, 20–21, 26–27, 40–41, 42–44, 46–47, 72, 75, 91–92, 94–95, 98–99, 101–3, 112, 123, 130

John Paul II, Saint, 1, 3, 6–7, 8, 134n2
Judaism, 71, 74, 75, 131

Kennedy, John F., 113n19, 138
Khrushchev, Nikita, 121, 129

Leo XIII (pope), 3n8, 14, 21, 23, 24, 118
liberalism, 31, 41, 43, 85–86, 99, 136
liturgy, 33, 69, 78, 87, 95–97, 109, 118, 127–28, 135
Luther, Martin, 43
Lutheranism, 43, 90, 98

Marxism, 92, 99, 100, 101. *See also* socialism; communism

mercy, 84, 86, 110, 111, 120, 125, 134–35, 137
missions, 46–48, 54, 60, 85
Montini, Giovanni Battista. *See* Paul VI (pope)

nationalism, 21, 41, 42, 46, 55, 59–60, 68, 69, 70, 71, 74, 78, 88
neoscholasticism, 135
"new theology." *See nouvelle theologie*
nouvelle theologie, 85–88, 89–90

obedience, 40, 48, 53, 62, 80, 91
Orthodox Churches, 55, 58, 61, 63, 65, 69, 70–71, 73, 74, 77, 111, 118, 122. *See also* Eastern Rite
Ostpolitik, 90, 130

Pacelli, Eugenio. *See* Pius XII (pope)
Paul VI (pope), 3–5, 90, 109n8
patristics, 48, 77, 96–97, 98, 135
peace, 39–40, 78, 80, 81–82, 104, 110, 111–12, 121–22, 126–27, 129, 130
Pius IX (pope), 3, 6, 7, 8, 12
Pius X (pope), 2, 3, 21, 24, 27, 34, 35, 37, 38, 45, 95, 120
Pius XI (pope), 3n8, 46, 52, 53, 70, 74, 102, 114
Pius XII (pope), 2, 3–5, 8, 26, 52, 70, 72, 74, 76, 82, 87,

90–91, 92, 104, 105, 107, 108, 114
politics, 7, 12–13, 20–21, 43, 47, 56, 60–61, 83–84, 89–90, 92, 98–102, 121–23, 130, 138
poverty, 11–12, 14, 40, 46–47, 62, 93, 120, 137

racism, 74, 75–76, 78. *See also* anti-Semitism
Radini Tedeschi, Giacomo Maria (cardinal), 29–32, 34–35, 37, 38–39, 41, 45, 53, 77
Ratti, Achille. *See* Pius XI (pope)
renewal. *See aggiornamento*
ressourcement, 17, 96–99, 135, 136
Roman Curia, 1, 3, 4n10, 35, 39, 47–48, 57, 63–67, 73, 103–4, 106–8, 111, 114–15, 119, 125, 127, 129, 138
Rome (city), 12–13, 20–21, 44–46, 116, 127
Rome (diocese), 20–21, 24, 35–36, 110, 115, 131
Roncalli family, 11–12, 13–14, 30, 41, 66, 95, 106, 120, 137
Russia, 5–6, 55, 76, 81, 99, 121–22, 129–30

saints, 1–10, 14, 15, 16, 17, 19, 22–23, 47, 52, 77, 97–98, 102, 113, 124, 133–34
Sarto, Giuseppe Melchiorre. *See* Pius X (pope)
Scripture, 95, 96, 98, 109, 128, 135, 136. *See also* Bible

Second Vatican Council, 4, 6, 88, 110–11, 114–17, 121–29, 136–37
secularization, 12–13, 68, 70–72, 77, 83, 86, 99, 138
seminary, 14, 15–20, 34, 39–40, 42, 77n40
Shoah, 5, 75, 116–17, 139
socialism, 43, 92, 99, 100, 101. *See also* Marxism
social Catholicism, 13, 14, 26–27, 29, 31, 35, 118
social teaching. *See* social Catholicism
Soviet Union. *See* Russia
spirituality, 15–20, 21–23, 36–37, 38, 40, 43–44, 64, 67, 78, 83, 86, 91, 104, 109, 113, 123–24, 134, 137, 138

Teresa of Ávila, Saint, 17, 21–22
Thomas à Kempis, 17, 113
Trent, Council of 12, 15, 31, 32, 62, 77n40, 98, 102–3, 136–37
Tridentinism. *See* Counter-Reformation

ultramontanism, 13
Uniatism, 58, 63
United States of America, 13, 23, 65, 112–13, 121, 138

Vatican II. *See* Councils, Second Vatican

Vianney, Saint John, 17

Wojtyła, Karol. *See* John
   Paul II, Saint
women, 16, 38, 42, 44
World War I, 40–44, 55, 58, 59,
   112, 135, 138

World War II, 5, 75–77, 79–80,
   82, 84, 92, 112, 116, 134,
   135, 138, 139

youth, 11–27, 41–42, 44, 88,
   113, 116, 134